THE SHORT GAME, DISTILLED

Illustrated Guide to Pitching, Chipping, Bunkers and Putting

PETE STYLES

The publisher Golf Distillery Inc. and the author Pete Styles cannot be held responsible for any injuries, which may occur as a result of these golf exercises. The publisher and author also disclaim any liability of any kind for losses or damages caused or alleged to be caused directly, or indirectly, from using the information contained herein.

Published by
Golf Distillery - Extracting the Essence of Golf

Copyright © 2025 Golf Distillery Inc.
All rights reserved.

Neither this guide, nor any parts within it may be sold or reproduced in any form without prior permission.

Ebook ISBN: 978-1-7381706-5-4
Paperback ISBN: 978-1-7381706-6-1
Hardcover ISBN: 978-1-7381706-7-8

TABLE OF CONTENTS

Introduction   v
The Short Game, Distilled   vii
Illustrated Guide to the Scoring Distance   ix

1 - PITCHING   1
1.1 Pitching Setup   3
1.2 Pitching Distance Control   10
1.3 Pitching Technique   17
1.4 Pitching Drill   21

2 - CHIPPING   27
2.1 Chipping Setup   29
2.2 Chipping Drill   39
2.3 Chipping Distance Control   45
2.4 Chipping Club Selection   51
2.5 How to Hit a Bump & Run   56
2.6 How to Hit a Flop Shot   61
2.7 How to Chip from a Downhill Lie   68
2.8 How to Chip from an Uphill Lie   73
2.9 How to Chip from a Tight Lie   78
2.10 How to Chip from the Rough   82
— Ball Buried Down in the Rough   84
— Ball Sitting Up in the Rough   88

3 - BUNKER SHOTS   93
3.1 Bunker Shot Setup   95
3.2 How Much Sand for Bunker Shots?   103
3.3 Bunker Shot Drill   107
3.4 Bunker Shot Distance Control   112
3.5 Bunker Shots from Compact or Wet Sand   117

3.6 Bunker Shots from a Plugged Lie	123
3.7 Bunker Shots from Sloping Lies	131
— Uphill Slope (Upslope)	132
— Downhill Slope (Downslope)	139
3.8 Fairway Bunker Shots	147
4 - PUTTING	157
4.1 Putting Alignment	160
4.2 Putting Stance & Ball Position	165
4.3 Putting Posture	171
4.4 Putting Grip	174
4.5 Putting Stroke	181
4.6 Putting Distance Control	188
4.7 Alternative Putting Grip Styles	194
4.8 Reading Greens	200
4.9 Putting with a Hybrid	206
4.10 Putting Drill for Short Putts	210
YouTube Channel Link	215
Also by Golf Distillery	217

INTRODUCTION

to the "Golf, Distilled" Series

I have a passionate belief that anyone can play consistently great golf. That belief comes from delivering thousands of lessons to players from every walk of life and at every level.

What I've found is that when you commit just a short amount of time to really ingraining the proven fundamentals of golf, it transforms your game.

Fundamentals might not be new. They might not seem exciting either — especially when you read about "magic moves" and "undiscovered swing secrets" in glossy magazines and elsewhere on the internet.

But mastering the fundamentals is exciting. Very exciting. Why? Because it delivers.

It gives you everything you want from the game – solid, crisp ball striking, booming drives that split the fairway in two, penetrating irons, masterful touch and feel and of course... consistency – in every area of your game.

I'm sure you already know that golfers can spend years chasing one gimmick after another without seeing any long-term improvement in their game. The irony is that if they just spent a fraction of that time mastering the key fundamentals of golf, they'd have a great swing... a swing for life.

That's the aim of this series of illustrated guides: to inspire you to become the great golfer you can be... and to give you step-by-step lessons to help achieve it!

Pete Styles, PGA Class A Professional
Over 75 000 lessons delivered
Manchester, England, UK

THE SHORT GAME, DISTILLED

ILLUSTRATED GUIDE TO THE SCORING DISTANCE

TIPS FOR PITCHING, CHIPPING, BUNKERS & PUTTING

What's the easiest way to knock shots off your golf handicap or improve your scores? I'll give you a clue. It's not hitting your drives an extra 20 yards.

You play the majority of your golf shots on or around the green, so why not practice that part of your game more? If you hit every shot from within 100 yards with the aim of the next shot being a makable putt then your scores will tumble.

Having a solid golf short game has the added advantage of taking some of the pressure off your approach play. If you think that you need to hit the green or it's a certain bogey, then more than likely you are going to miss the green. If you think that even if you miss the green you've got a decent shot at getting up and down then you take the pressure off your approach shots and play a smoother stroke, more likely to succeed.

In this guide I'll cover the lessons and tips you need in order to:

- Pitch on to the green
- Chip close to the flag
- Master bunker shots
- Sink more putts

1 - PITCHING

Pitching and chipping are often rolled into one but I've split them into two separate sections.

For clarification, any shot that requires less than a full swing — typically anything under 80-100 yards — we'll call a pitch shot. And anything around the fringes or the apron of the green — about 25 yards and in from the pin — we'll call a chip shot.

The lessons in this first section will help you hit short approach shots onto the green. If you do happen to miss the green, we'll cover chipping and bunker play in the next two sections.

1.1 PITCHING SETUP

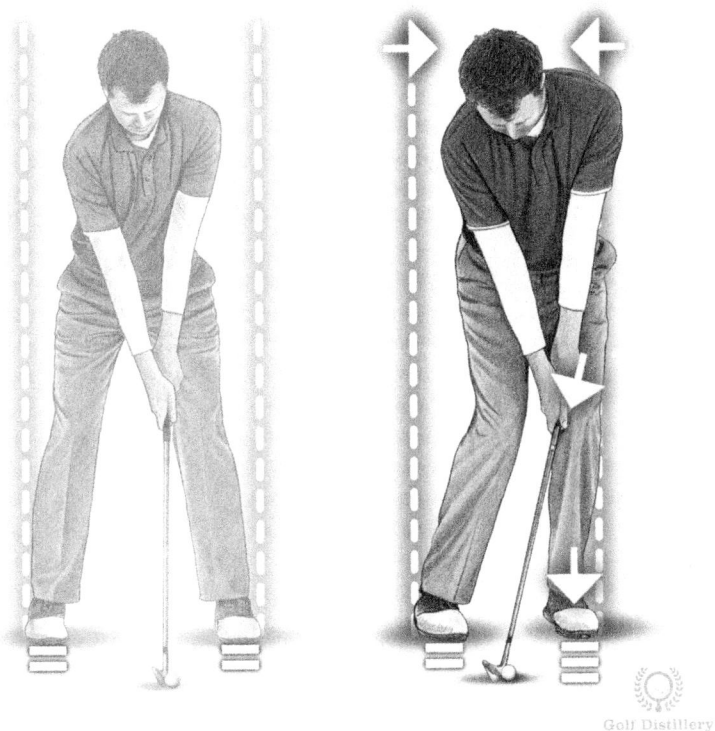

Learning how to hit pitch shots with both accuracy and consistency will have a major impact on your golf game.

It's a great confidence booster to know that if you hit a wayward drive and can't make the green in two, you still have a good chance of saving par because your pitching is so good.

Pitching should be a skill that most golfers can master to a very reasonable level of competence. That's because it requires less timing and coordination compared to full swings or drives and less physical strength and flexibility as well.

However, most amateur golfers lack confidence over their pitch shots and are happy to land the ball anywhere on the green.

In this first lesson we'll start with the proper pitch shot setup.

- For a pitch shot, start with the same good setup that you use for full swings. However, we now want to replace the elements that help generate power and replace them with elements that promote feel and control.

- You can reduce power and increase control on a sliding scale — which will help with your distance control — by adjusting the following elements of your setup:

1. Width of stance
2. How low you grip your club
3. Length of swing

- With your lob wedge for example, a full shoulder-width stance, gripping the club at the top of the grip and a full swing might send the ball 65 yards (A). Gripping halfway down the grip, narrowing your stance and taking a 3/4 swing might send the ball 50 yards (B). Finally, gripping right at the bottom of the grip, with a narrow stance and a half swing might fly the ball 35 yards (C).

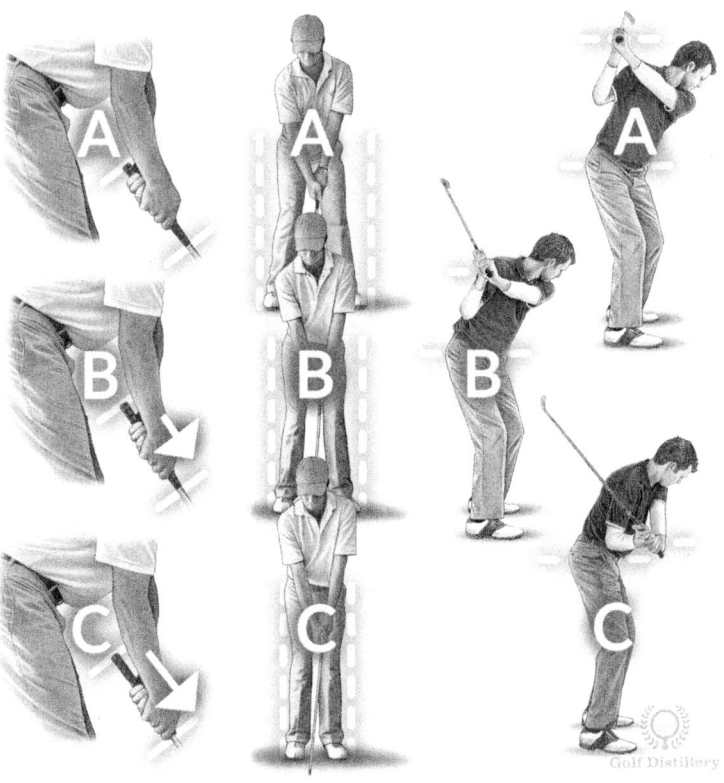

1 - PITCHING

- Hit some balls at the range with these three setup positions and with three different clubs — ideally gap wedge, sand wedge and lob wedge. That will give you nine pitch shot distances. We'll take this a step further in the next lesson.

- For shorter pitch shots where you're taking a narrow stance and gripping right down the club, you should also open your stance (feet and hips pointing left of target for the right-handed golfer). Also, place more weight on your front side —about 60/40 favouring your front foot.

1.2 PITCHING DISTANCE CONTROL

Pitching and chipping — especially when it comes to distance control — are said to be very much down to feel and finesse. Unfortunately, developing a high degree of feel can take years of practice. But I'd like to show you how to leapfrog that learning curve somewhat by taking a more structured approach to your pitch shots.

To shorten the time you need to improve your pitching distance control, complete the following exercise.

- Take three lofted clubs to the practice range — ideally a gap wedge, a sand wedge and a lob wedge.

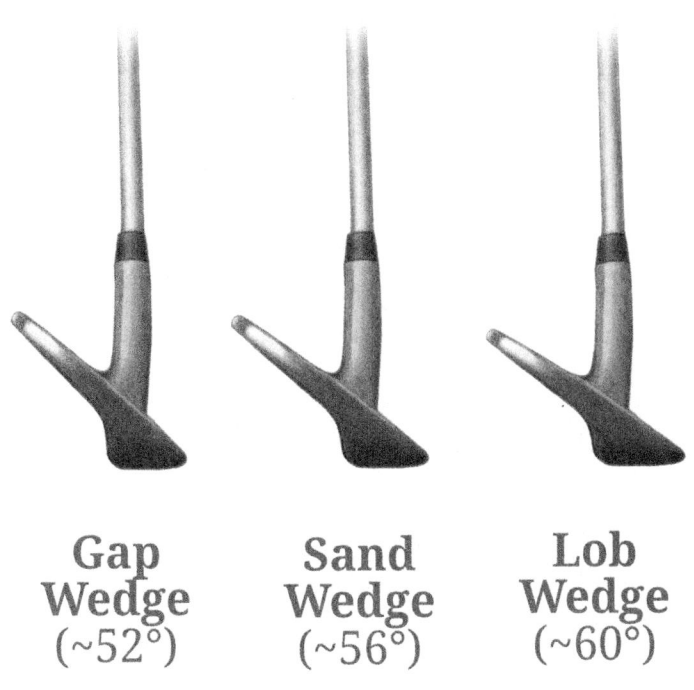

Gap Wedge (~52°) **Sand Wedge** (~56°) **Lob Wedge** (~60°)

- **[A]** Take your most lofted club —lob wedge if you have it — and hit ten full shots with the club parallel to the ground behind your head. However, grip down the club slightly and take a slightly narrower stance than you normally would for a full shot. Pace out the average distance of those ten shots.

- **[B]** Now hit ten more pitch shots but this time only taking the club back until your arms are parallel to the ground. Also, grip further down the club and take a narrower stance. Pace out the average distance of those ten shots.

- **{C}** Finally, hit ten pitch shots with a short backswing — only until your hands are at hips level (or clubhead at head level). You should be gripping right down the club with the narrowest stance. Pace out the average distance of those ten shots.

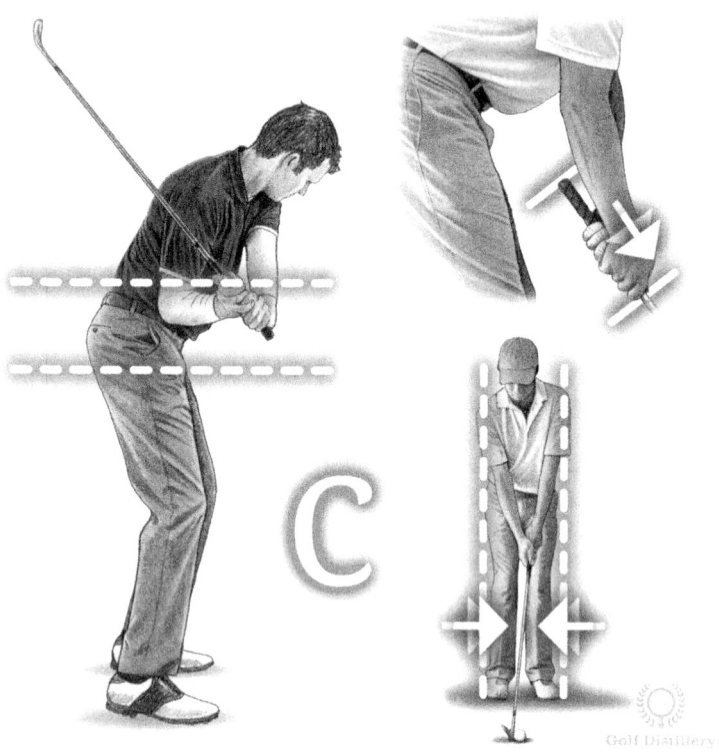

- Repeat this sequence of A-B-C adjustments while using your other two clubs.

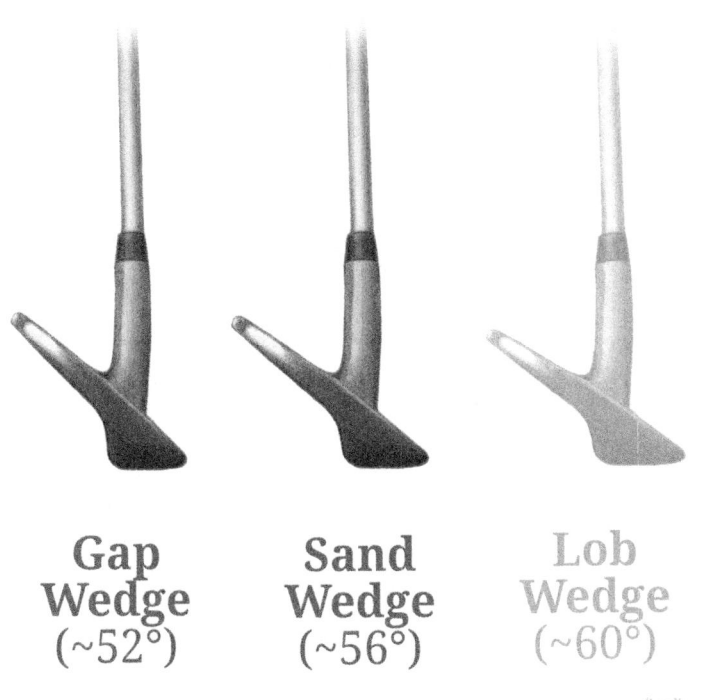

Gap Wedge (~52°)   **Sand Wedge (~56°)**   **Lob Wedge (~60°)**

- You should now have nine distances fairly evenly spaced apart. Memorize these or write them on a piece of paper for quick reference. On the golf course, determine how far your target is and use the appropriate combination of club and length of backswing that will get you closest. Make a few practice swings and go ahead and hit the shot.

--- Pitching Distances ---

	Gap Wedge (~52°)	Sand Wedge (~56°)	Lob Wedge (~60°)
A	?	?	?
B	?	?	?
C	?	?	?

1.3 PITCHING TECHNIQUE

If you want to improve the quality and consistency of your pitch shots focus on hitting the ball down into the ground.

One of the most common short game faults amongst handicap golfers is trying to 'help' pitch and chip shots into the air with a scooping action of the hands.

But even if you don't think you're guilty of that scooping wrist action, I'd be willing to bet you don't consciously hit down on the ball as much as you should.

Consider the following lesson for help on how to avoid fat and thin mishits. You should end up striking the ball with greater consistency and control.

- Place more weight on your front side (on your left foot for the right-handed golfer) at setup and as you follow through.

- Feel as though you are keeping your right hand on top of the golf ball through impact. This is a very different sensation to throwing a ball up in the air for example, where your right hand would be underneath the ball launching it upwards.

1 - PITCHING

- Trust the loft on your club. Keeping your right hand on top of the ball through impact might feel as though you'll hit it too low but the ball will roll up the face of the club, generating plenty of height and some backspin.

1.4 PITCHING DRILL

This drill will help prevent fluffed pitch shots. It stops you from decelerating through the ball and promotes a solid, crisp strike instead.

Decelerating through the ball is a common issue and I think it often occurs as a result of a backswing that is too long.

From a long backswing you can feel like you have too much power and that you're going to fly the ball through the back of the green, especially if you catch it a bit thin. You then unconsciously decelerate during the downswing to try and compensate. But because the clubhead is quite heavy, it overtakes the hands causing a scooping action. The final result? A fat or thin contact.

The solution is to take a shorter backswing and focus on really accelerating through the ball, as I break down in this lesson.

- Keep your backswing relatively compact and short — less than you think you need for the distance of the shot.

- Really accelerate through the ball to generate the correct power and distance for the shot.

- A good rule of thumb is a one-third backswing, two-thirds follow through. Essentially, your follow through should be twice the length of your backswing.

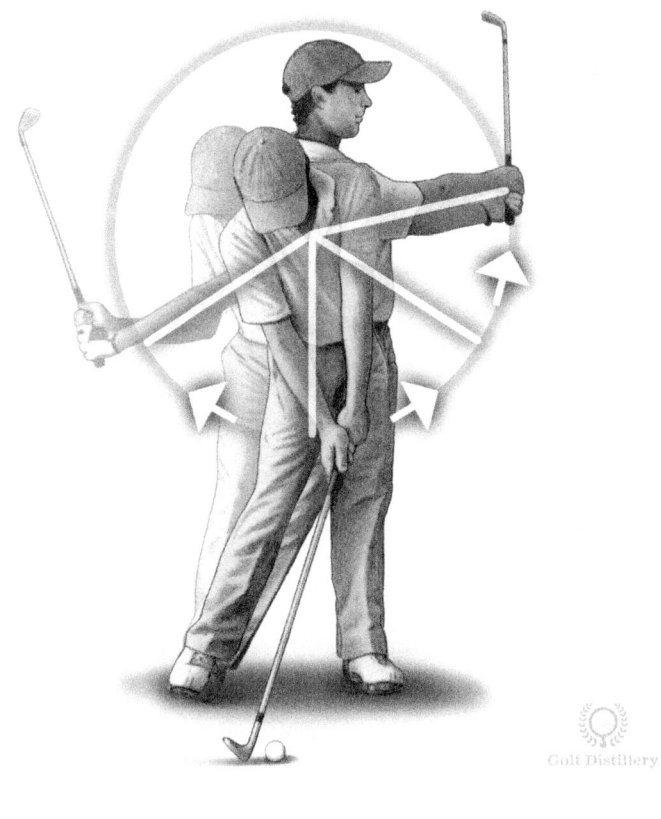

2 - CHIPPING

In contrast to a pitch shot and for the sake of clarification, let's assume that any shot around the apron of the green within about 25 yards of the pin is a chip shot.

In this chipping section of the guide we'll cover the fundamentals of a correct setup, distance control and club selection. Taken together they'll help you to develop solid chipping skills and good, consistent ball striking.

We'll also look at some more advanced techniques, such as chipping from sloping, bare, or rough lies as well as some chip shot variations such as the flop shot and the chip & run.

Finally, we'll also look at ways to shield you from thinning or topping your chip shots.

2.1 CHIPPING SETUP

In this first lesson we'll look at how to set up for chip shots.

Because chipping is all about feel and similarly to pitching, we want to replace any elements of our setup that are designed to generate power and replace them with elements that generate more control.

Adjusting your stance, grip and bodyweight at setup will help you achieve this, as well as some simple swing thoughts.

Even if you're not able to work on your chipping technique next to a suitable practice green I'd encourage you to rehearse your chipping setup and swing at home. Even by just brushing a carpet with the clubhead you'll build confidence and consistency so that a good chipping action and ball strike becomes second nature on the golf course.

Let's begin.

- To chip the golf ball we don't need power, we need control. Similarly to pitching, adjusting your grip, stance and bodyweight relative to a full swing set up will help you achieve more control.

- Take a narrow stance. For most golfers, I don't advocate putting your feet all the way together as it leads to poor balance. A stance similar to what you might take standing in line is a good rule of thumb.

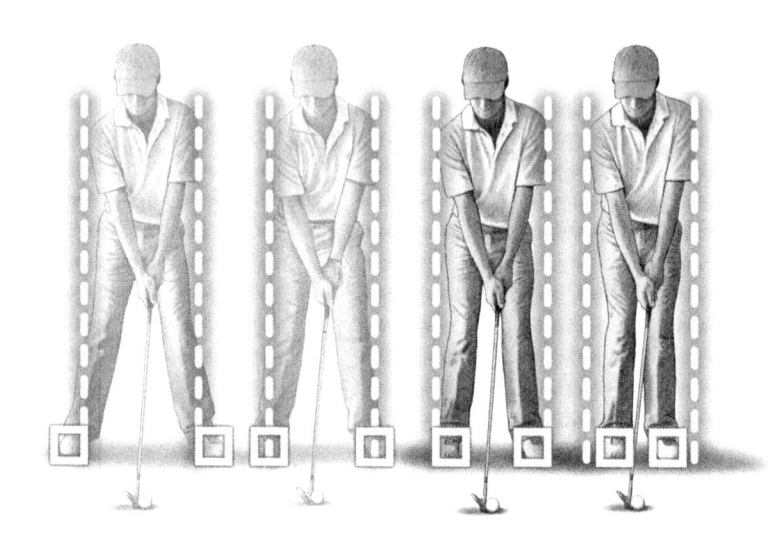

- Gripping the club at the top generates the most power. In order to favour control instead, feel free to grip right down the club so that your bottom hand is touching the metal of the shaft.

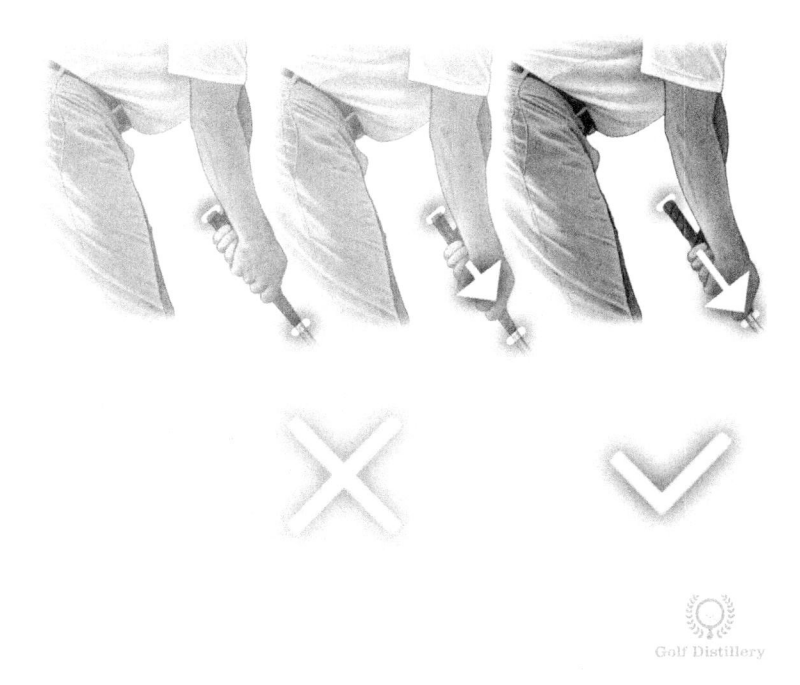

- When chipping, we want to recreate the impact position of full speed swings during our setup. Specifically, at impact the hips are open and the bodyweight is forward on to the front side. So at address, aim your feet and hips left of target (for the right-handed golfer).

- Your shoulders should still point to the target — not left. This will allow the swing path to stay on a good line towards the pin but your hips and legs won't obstruct your swing.

- Address the ball with about 70% of your weight on your front leg.

- Your hands should be well forward of the ball in such a way that the club shaft points to your left hip.

- Finally, raising your rear heel slightly through impact will prevent you from keeping too much weight on the back foot — a surefire way to mishit the golf ball fat or thin.

2.2 CHIPPING DRILL

This drill should help improve the consistency of your chips. It should also improve another important element of your chipping in the distance control — one of the keys to successful chipping. And the basis of good distance control is a chipping action that is consistently repeatable.

When you have a simple, repeatable chipping action, you can simply make a slightly shorter or longer backswing or select a different club and still get reliable, accurate results. And a good chipping action should be dominated by the shoulders and the upper body, almost like a long putting stroke.

The biggest cause of fat and thin chip mishits is what I call 'flicky' wrists — a slight scooping motion that tries to help the ball in the air.

It may not be obvious to you but if your chipping ball striking is inconsistent, it's probably due to too much wrist motion. That's why for most golfers I recommend keeping the hands relatively quiet and passive during chip shots — very little wrist hinging, similar to a putting action.

Try the following drill to really highlight any flicking or scooping tendencies in your chipping motion.

- Set up as normal and then slide your hands right down to the bottom of the club – near the clubhead. The shaft of the club should be running past your left hip (for the right-handed golfer).

- With your hands in that position make a short backswing and follow through.

- As you follow through, the club shaft should stay well away from your left side. In other words, it should NOT hit your left hip. Any releasing of the wrists will cause the club to strike your left side.

- You might be surprised by just how much you have to prevent the wrists from hinging in order to prevent the club shaft from touching you. Try to recreate this feeling and motion during your normal chip shots.

2.3 CHIPPING DISTANCE CONTROL

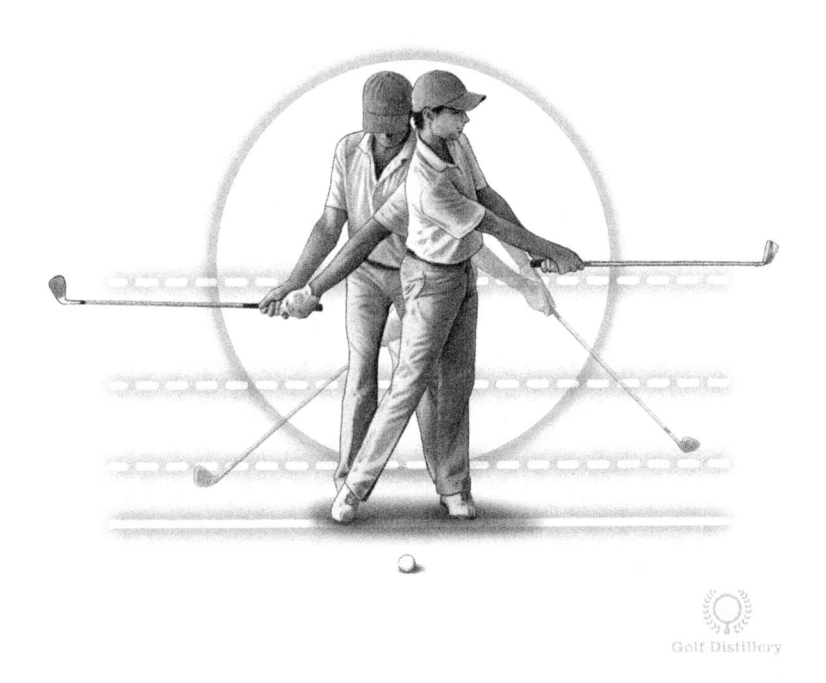

Once you're happy with your chipping setup and basic technique we can look at how you can achieve good distance control.

Chipping — and putting — distance control is very much about 'feel' but a high level of feel can take hours and hours of practice to develop.

One way you can significantly shorten the learning curve

is to take a more structured approach to your chipping game, as I explain in this lesson.

- Take a lofted club — like a pitching wedge — and adopt a good chipping address position.

PW

- **[A]** Take a short backswing so that the clubhead reaches about **ankle height** and follow through to the same height. Chip 5-10 golf balls and pace out the average distance.

- **[B]** Repeat the process but taking the clubhead back to **knee height** and through to knee height after impact.

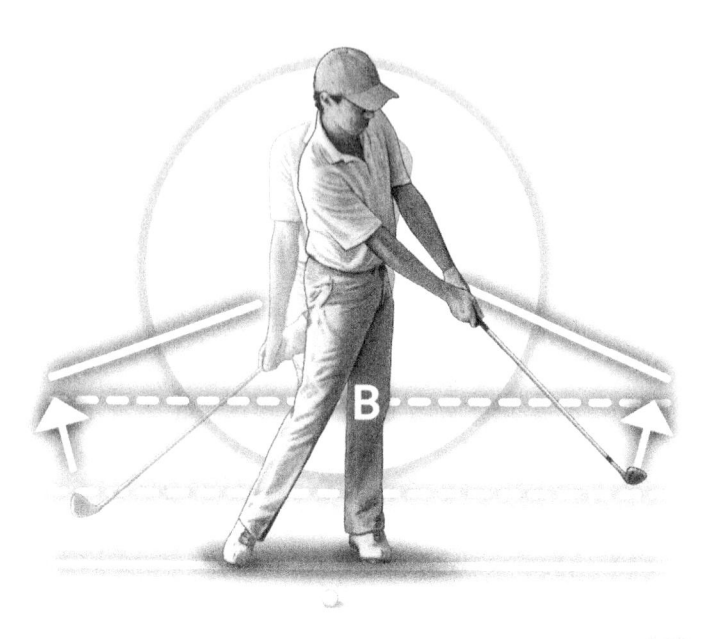

- **[C]** Repeat the process once more, taking the club back and through to **hip height**.

- This will give you three chipping distances around the green. Repeat this with two other clubs — ideally a lob wedge and an 8-iron — to give yourself nine different distances. It can be helpful to write these down for easy reference when out on the course.

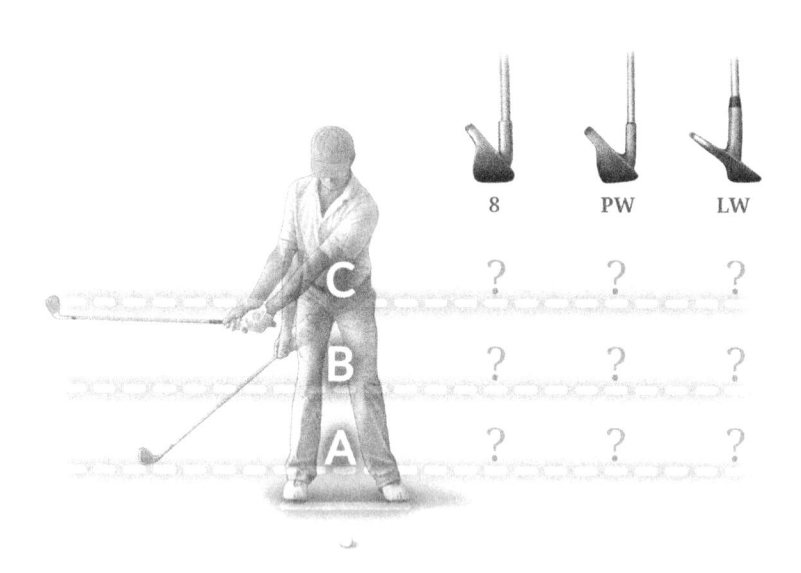

- - - Chipping Distances - - -

2.4 CHIPPING CLUB SELECTION

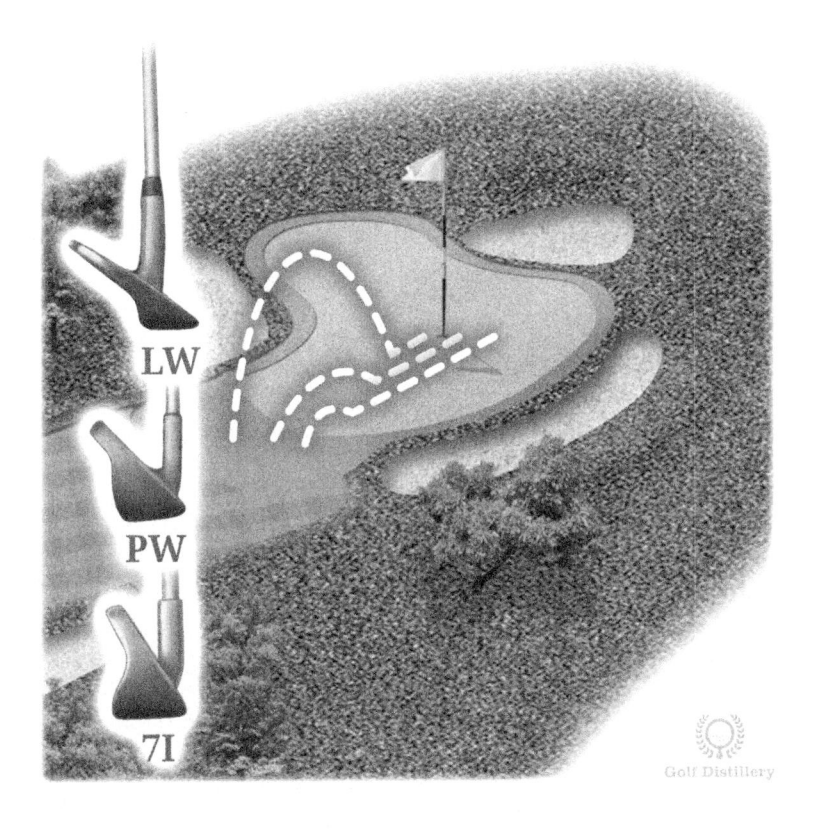

A quick recap. In the first lesson of this section we looked at setting up correctly for chip shots.

In the second lesson we reviewed a useful drill that helps develop a solid, repeatable chipping action. And finally, in the third lesson we looked at the correct technique for distance control.

In this fourth lesson we'll look at club selection for chips and how various lofts (clubs) affect the flight-to-roll ratios.

- Using the most lofted wedge in my bag — a 60-degree lob wedge — the ball should spend most of its distance in the air and stop relatively quickly (approx. fly 70-80% of the total distance).

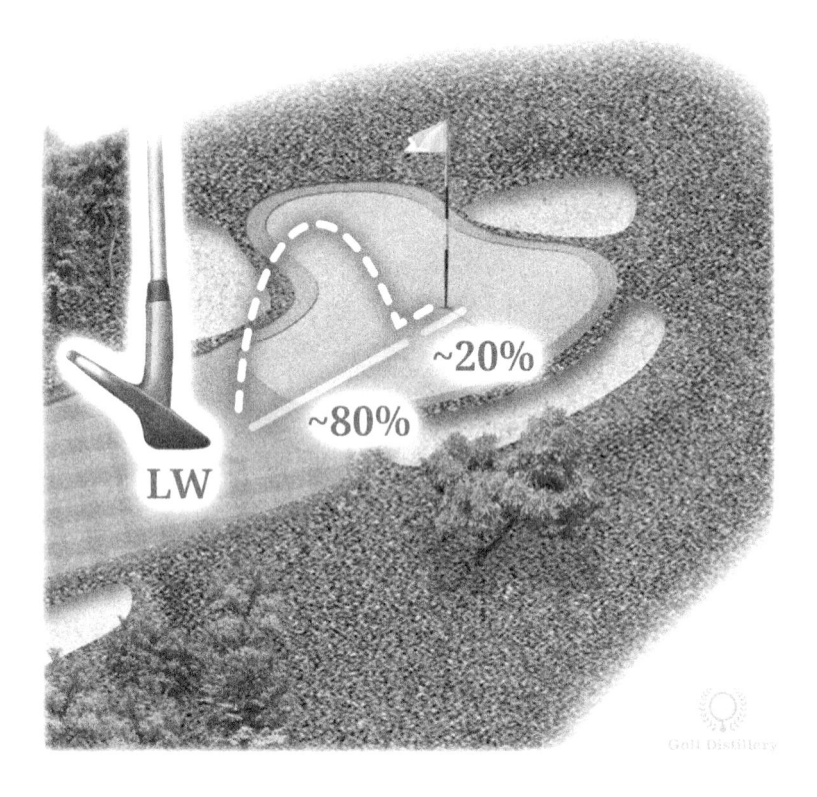

- Switching to a pitching wedge, we'd expect the ball to fly about 50% of the distance and roll the remaining 50%. With that club we'll need to make a shorter chipping action because more of the power is transferred into forward momentum rather than getting the ball in the air.

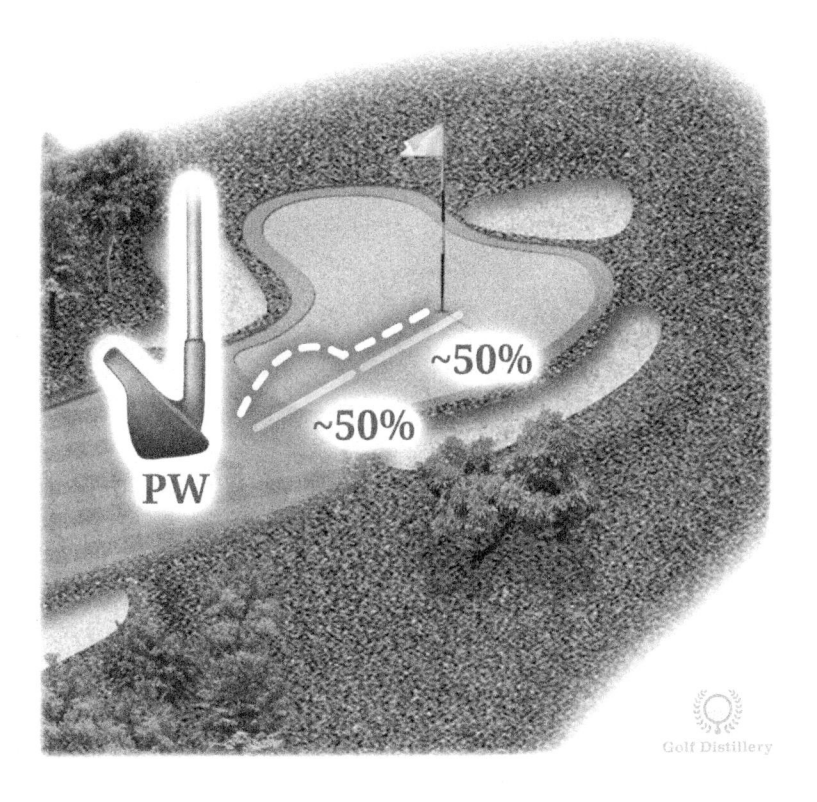

- Taking a 7-iron, the ball should fly only about 20% of the distance and roll the remaining 80%. We'll make a very short chipping action because nearly all the power is transferred into forward momentum.

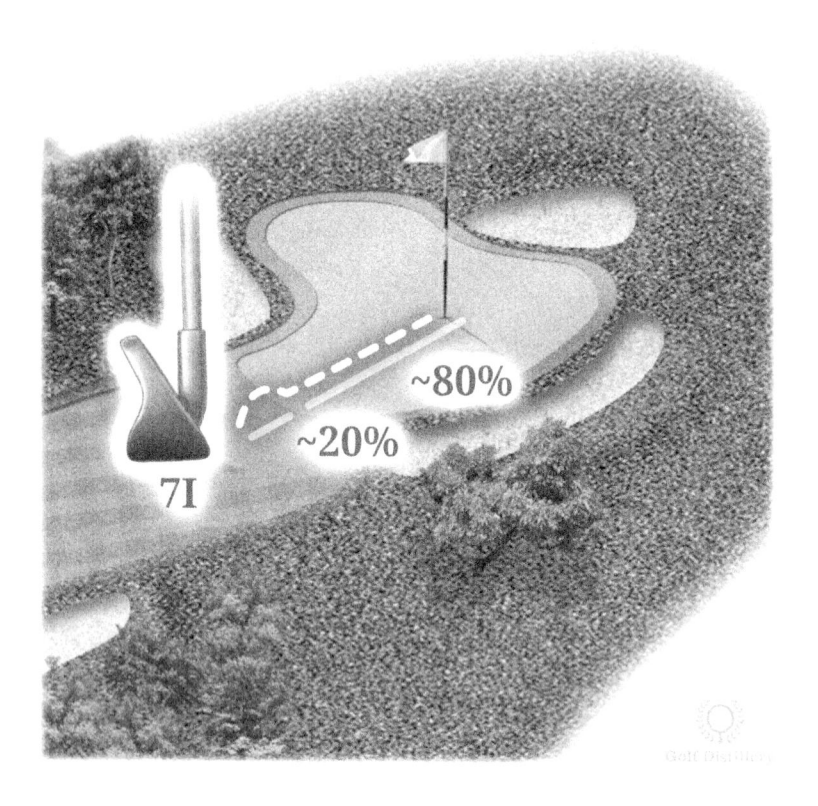

- Regardless of the club you select, the setup and chipping action is the same. The only variables are the length of backswing and the club in hand.

2.5 HOW TO HIT A BUMP & RUN

We'll now begin to explore modifications to the basic chip shot in order to better face the various situations you will encounter on the golf course.

The bump and run is a very useful shot option when you don't have any hazards between you and the pin and when the fairway is quite flat and closely mown.

It's also what I would call a percentage shot. That's because a poorly struck chip and run shot often elicits a similar result to a well struck one. On the other hand, a badly hit flop shot using a lob wedge, which we'll cover next, can be disastrous.

- A chip with a lofted club requires a much longer backswing because a lot of the energy is used in giving the ball height. Generally speaking the longer the backswing, the more potential there is for a mishit and those mishits tend to travel a lot further.

LW

- A chip with a lower lofted club — like a 7 or 8-iron — requires a much shorter backswing because most of the energy is transferred into forward momentum. A shorter backswing also makes it easier to get a perfect strike on the ball and the results of a thin contact won't be too dissimilar.

- Otherwise, use a normal chipping setup and technique for the chip and run.

2.6 HOW TO HIT A FLOP SHOT

The flop shot is a very useful option when you have a hazard between you and the pin and little green to work with. Executed correctly, you'll be able to stop the ball very quickly and give yourself a good chance of getting up and down. However, there are a couple of caveats to bear in mind.

Firstly, remember that poor course management skills cost club-level golfers far more shots than an inability to play the flop shot. In other words, if you're not really confident over this shot — you haven't spent time practicing it — then take your medicine and choose a more prudent shot option.

Secondly, if you have anything other than a very good lie then opt for a safer shot.

With that in mind here is how you play a flop shot.

- Take the most lofted club in your bag — ideally a -60-degree lob wedge.

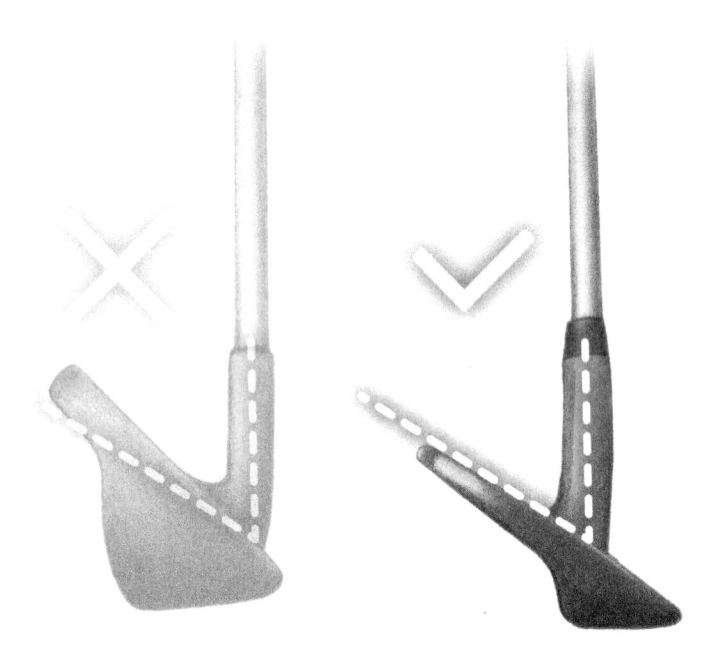

- Play the ball from the middle of your stance, or slightly forward.

- Open the club so that you feel as though you could balance a wine glass on the clubface.

- The clubface will be aiming well right of the target (for the right-handed golfer) so aim your feet, hips and shoulders well left to compensate.

- This setup position will lead to a very steep, out-to-in swing path but the ball should fly on quite a high, straight path towards your target.

- When practicing this shot, place a club along the line of the clubface that aims well right of target and one that aims along the line of your feet, well left of target. Focus on swinging the club along the line of your feet and trust that the open clubface will send the ball towards the pin.

2.7 HOW TO CHIP FROM A DOWNHILL LIE

The following few lessons will show you how to chip from awkward lies. And this first lesson shows you how to chip from a downhill sloping lie.

Imagine you've hit an approach shot on to the green and the ball has rolled up quite a severe slope at the back edge of the green. You now have a downhill lie that is going to affect the flight of the ball and also how you should set up.

Here are the adjustments you need to make in order to chip from a downslope.

- Take a normal, good chip shot setup. Now adjust the distance between your two feet by taking a slightly wider stance to help your balance.

- Tip your shoulders forward so that they run parallel to the line of the slope. Your spine should be at right angles — perpendicular — to the slope.

- Keep your weight predominantly on your front leg. Too much weight on the back foot can lead to thin and fat mishits. Be careful however that you don't lose your balance during the follow through.

2 - CHIPPING

- A downslope will have the effect of reducing the loft of your club. To compensate, I recommend you always opt for the most lofted club in your bag — a lob or sand wedge for example — when chipping from a downhill lie.

2.8 HOW TO CHIP FROM AN UPHILL LIE

For the flip side of the previous situation we'll now look at playing chip shots from an upslope.

One of the most common faults I see amongst club-level golfers is that they don't compensate for the slope by taking a lower lofted club — they still opt for the lob or sand wedge. Remember, an uphill lie will have the effect of adding loft to the club.

Here are the main points to remember.

- Take a normal, good chip shot setup. Adjust the distance between your feet by taking a slightly wider stance to help your balance.

- Tip your shoulders back so that they are aligned to the slope. Your spine should be at right angles — perpendicular — to the slope.

- You'll naturally feel more weight on your back foot. However, it's important to keep your bodyweight travelling forward through impact on to your left side. Keeping your weight on the back foot can knock you off balance and cause you to mishit the ball fat or thin.

- An upslope will have the effect of increasing the loft on your club. To compensate, take a lower lofted club than normal. A lob or sand wedge is probably not the best choice here as you'll need a lot of confidence to hit the ball quite hard for it to travel all the way to the hole.

2.9 HOW TO CHIP FROM A TIGHT LIE

Now that we have reviewed how to play chip shots from uneven lies the next few advanced lessons will focus on the actual grass conditions under the ball. Specifically, we'll look at bare/tight lies and heavy lies.

Bare or tight lies are notoriously difficult to chip from because it's so easy to mishit the ball thin. And thin chips are fairly destructive because they travel a long way. That explains why most amateur golfers play this shot with much trepidation.

Focus on the following in order to chip confidently from tight lies.

- Play the golf ball back in your stance, almost off the back foot. This will help you to strike down on the ball a little bit more, reducing the chances of a thin contact.

- I recommend you play a chip and run (bump and run) shot from a bare lie wherever possible. A chip and run shot with a 7-iron requires a shorter backswing and less power than a chip with a lob wedge. A poorly struck chip and run will produce results similar to a well struck one. On the other hand, a poorly struck lob wedge — that requires a much longer backswing — will usually end up costing you shots.

- Keep the bodyweight predominantly — around 70% — on the front foot. Your hands should be well ahead of the ball with the club shaft pointing into your left hip.

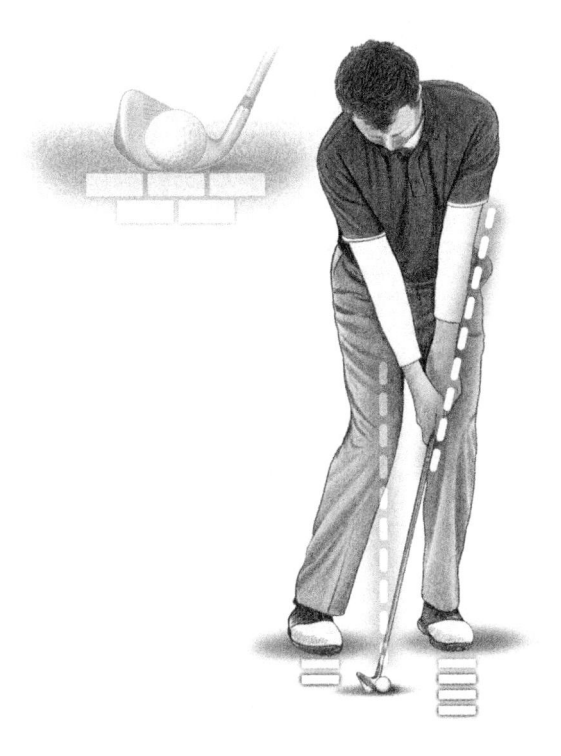

2.10 HOW TO CHIP FROM THE ROUGH

In this final lesson of the section I'd like to cover some tips for chipping the golf ball out of a heavy lie.

I actually cover two types of heavy lies because the way they are played is quite different.

When you find your ball in long grass around the fringes of the green, take a good look at how the ball is sitting. Get a feel for the length of the grass and how much is going to be underneath the ball. Then proceed accordingly with the following pointers in mind.

– BALL BURIED DOWN IN THE ROUGH

- The most important factor here is getting a good contact on the ball. We don't want the club to come into the thick grass too early because that will prevent you from getting any spin or from controlling the distance of the shot.

- Play the ball towards the back of your stance, certainly back of centre. Bodyweight and hands should be forward as usual with the feet and hips open.

- Unlike standard chip shots we want to see quite a lot of wrist hinge and for that wrist hinge to occur quite early in the backswing. You're aiming for a chopping action. A good swing thought is to point your thumbs to the sky very early in the takeaway.

- Finally, open the clubface quite significantly, almost as much as you would for a flop shot.

– BALL SITTING UP IN THE ROUGH

- This shot can seem a lot easier but be careful. Many golfers end up getting their clubhead right underneath the ball so it literally travels nowhere.

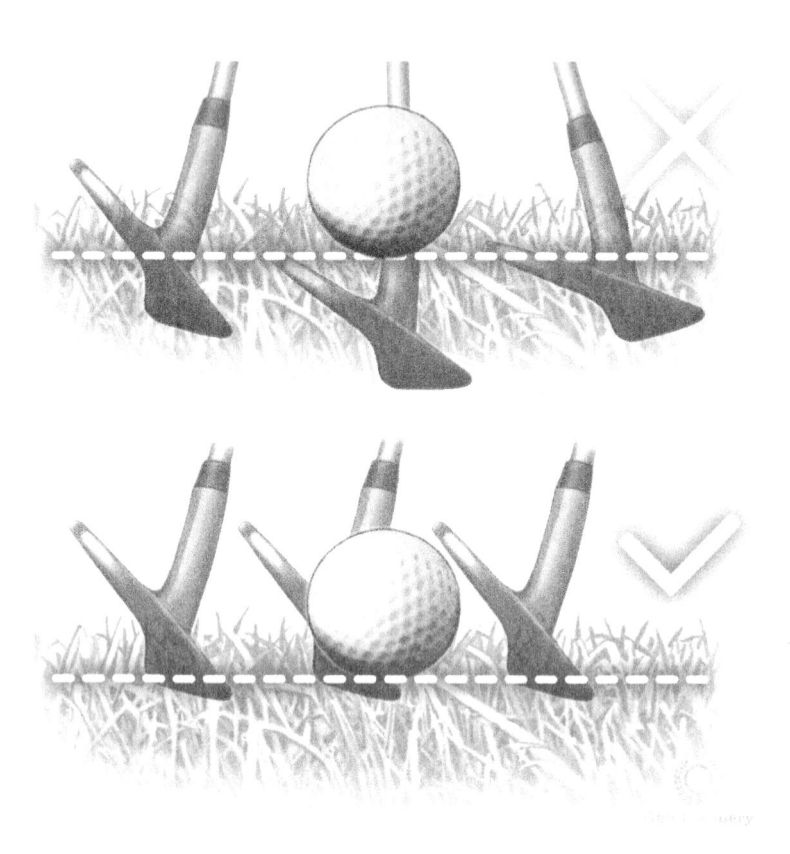

- Keep the club square — don't open the face, in contrast to the previous shot.

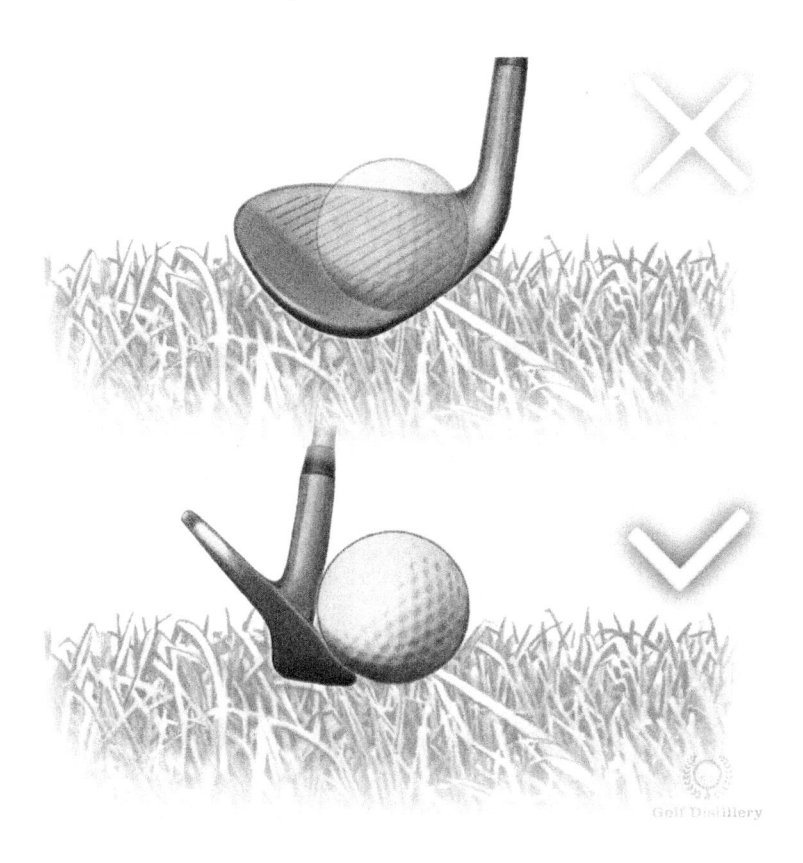

- Play the ball from the centre of your stance.

- Remove the aggressive and early wrist hinge of the previous ball buried situation. The hands and wrists should stay fairly passive for this chip shot.

- Go ahead and play the shot with confidence.

3 - BUNKER SHOTS

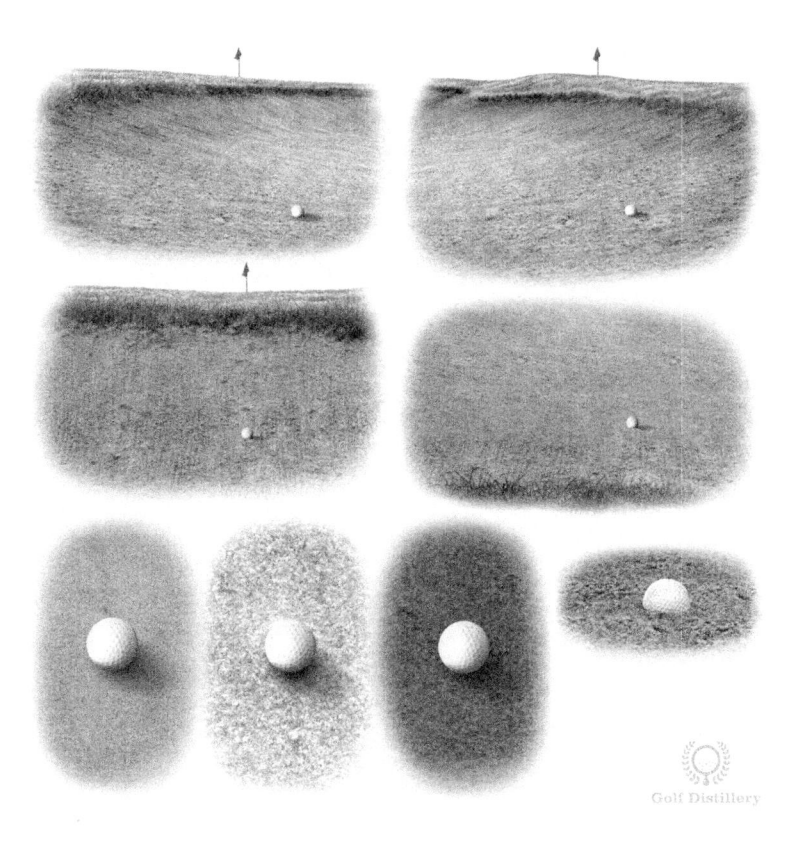

Bunker play seems to be the bane of the life of most amateur golfers. Statistics show that high handicappers rarely make 'sand saves', meaning they rarely get up and down from a greenside bunker.

But even those with a lower handicap struggle. A study of over 100 amateur golfers found that players with a handicap of 9 managed to get up and down from the sand just 7% of the time. And they were only slightly better than the 18-36 handicappers.

What's interesting is that golfers with a handicap of 5 were able to get up and down much more often — about 30% of the time. Also, they rarely left a ball in the bunker.

When quizzed, these 5-handicappers said they spent very little time practicing bunker shots. So what does that suggest? That just a small amount of practice initially — to ingrain good technique — should eventually reap quite big rewards on the golf course.

The bunker play lessons in this section of the guide should help turn you into a solid, consistent sand trap golfer. Hopefully, you'll progress from hardly ever getting up and down to making a sand save for one in every three bunkers you land in.

3.1 BUNKER SHOT SETUP

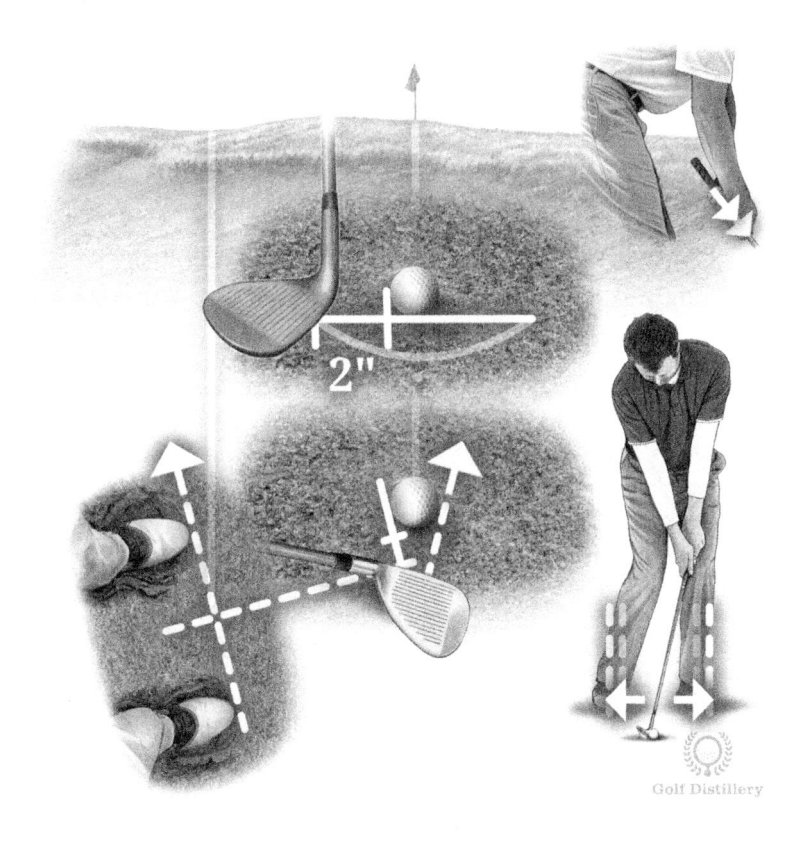

In this first lesson we'll look at the bunker shot setup. We'll then move on to the basic technique, distance control, a great drill and finally tips for more advanced bunker shots.

As you will see, the setup for bunker shots is similar to that of the pitching and chipping we have reviewed in the previous two sections.

3 - BUNKER SHOTS

Again here, the aim is to replace elements in the swing that generate power in favour of elements that generate control and feel.

- Take a slightly wider stance than you would for a chip shot — about shoulder width is good — and shuffle your feet into the sand so that you're standing on a flat, stable surface.

- Open the clubface so that it faces the sky — as though you could balance a wine glass on it.

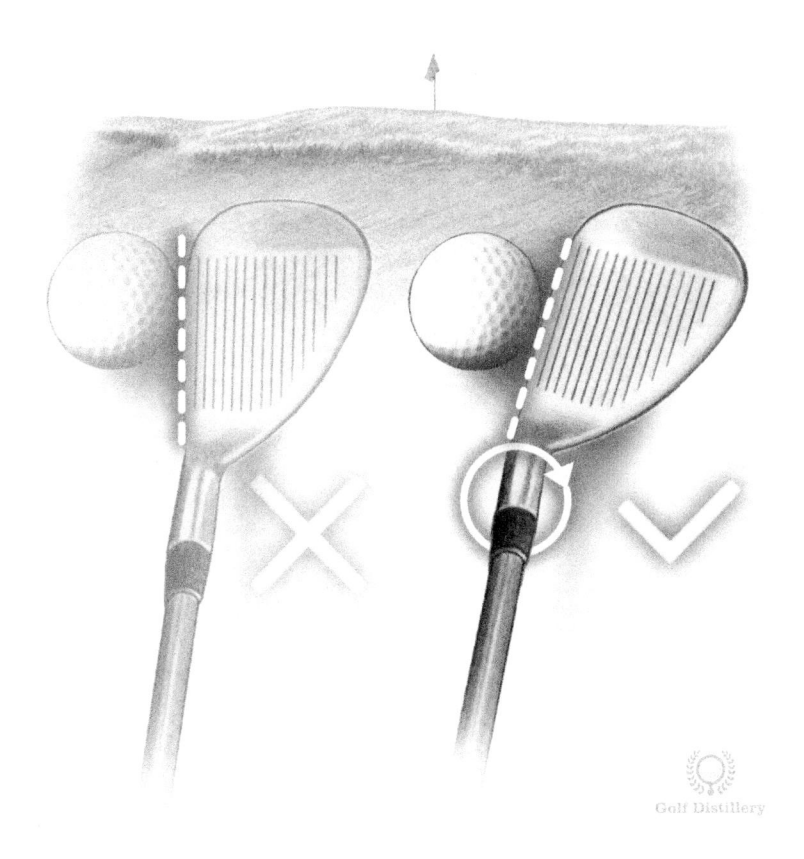

- Aim your feet and hips to the left of target (for the right-handed golfer) to compensate for the open clubface, which is pointing to the right of the target.

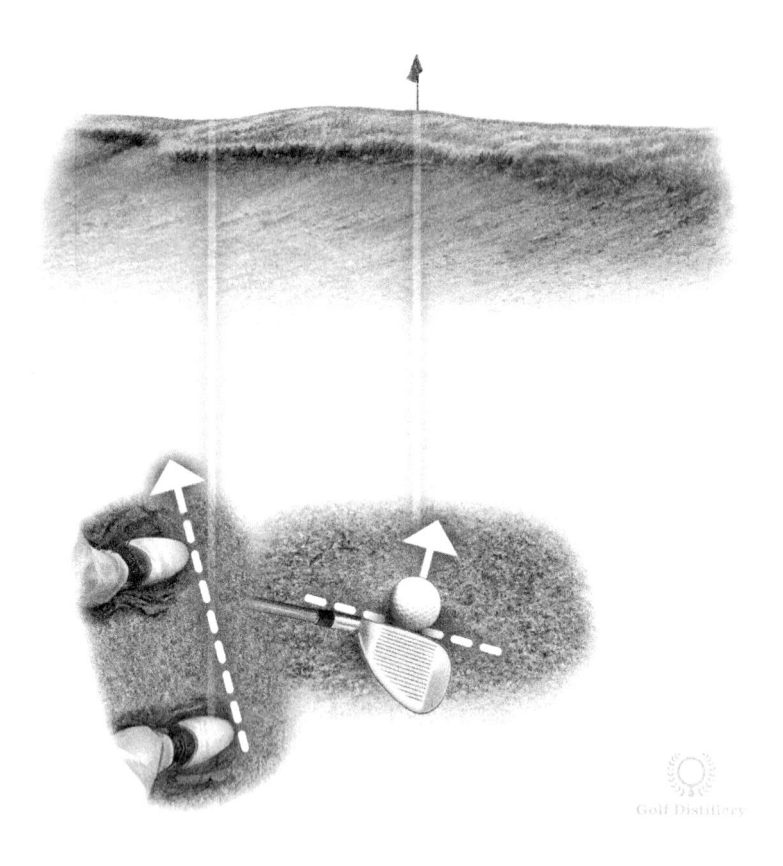

- Grip down towards the bottom of the grip for more control.

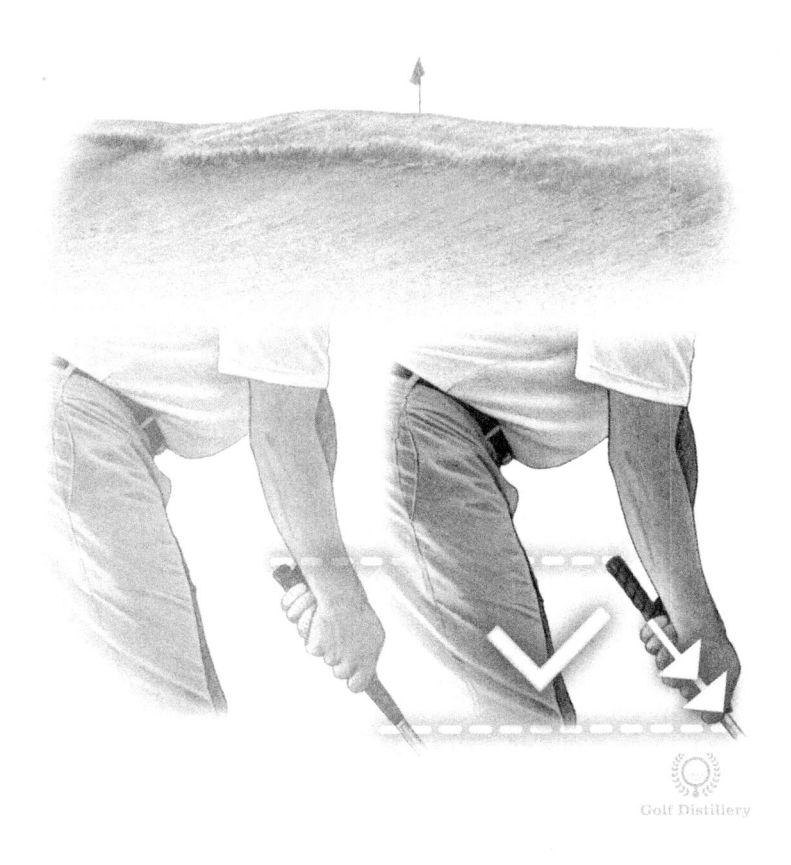

- The ball should be slightly ahead of centre in your stance. If you draw a line in the sand right in the middle of your stance, this is where the club should strike. The ball should be two inches ahead of that line.

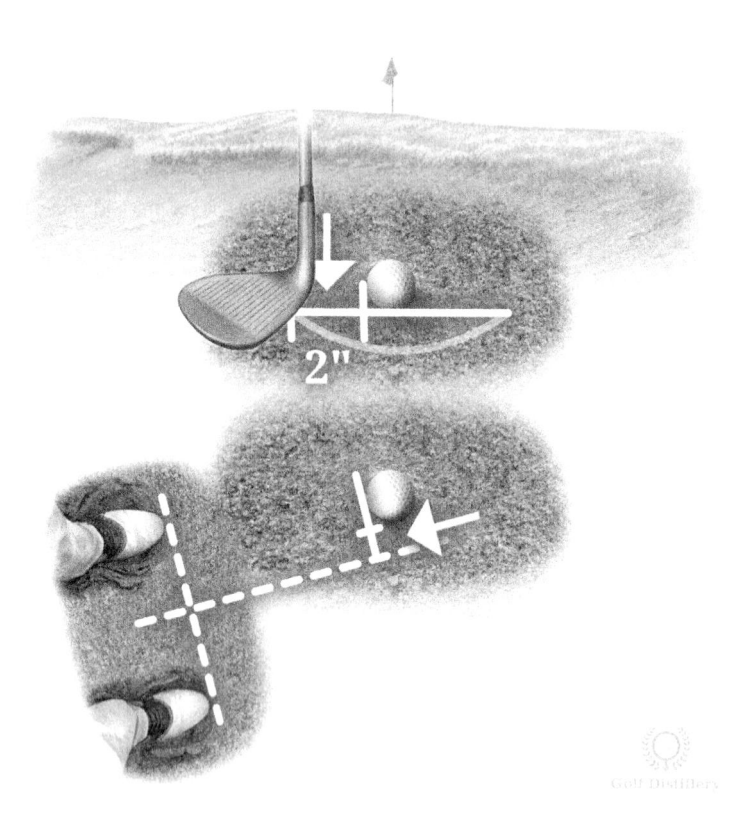

- Not every bunker shot has to be played with a full swing. Just as you would vary the length of your swing when chipping and pitching, you should for bunker shots too.

- Make a good follow through, accelerating through the golf ball. If you tend to decelerate and 'quit' on bunker shots, try making a one-third backswing and two-thirds follow through.

3.2 HOW MUCH SAND FOR BUNKER SHOTS?

Now, once you're comfortable with setting up correctly for bunker shots let's look at getting a good, consistent strike in the sand.

Most golfers appreciate that they need to strike the sand before the golf ball. But I think a fear of hitting the ball thin and seeing it shoot off over the other side of the green causes them to consistently take too much sand. Combine that with the classic mistake of decelerating through the ball and more often than not the golf ball stays in the bunker.

Just remember the following simple lesson.

- Aim to strike the sand two inches behind the ball.

- Pick a spot in the sand behind the ball — rather than the ball itself — and focus on this point of impact during your swing.

- A good-sized divot in the sand is about six inches in length. Specifically, it should start two inches before the ball and end four inches after. It should also be an inch or two deep. Any more sand than this and it becomes very difficult to get the ball out of the bunker without making a very aggressive swing.

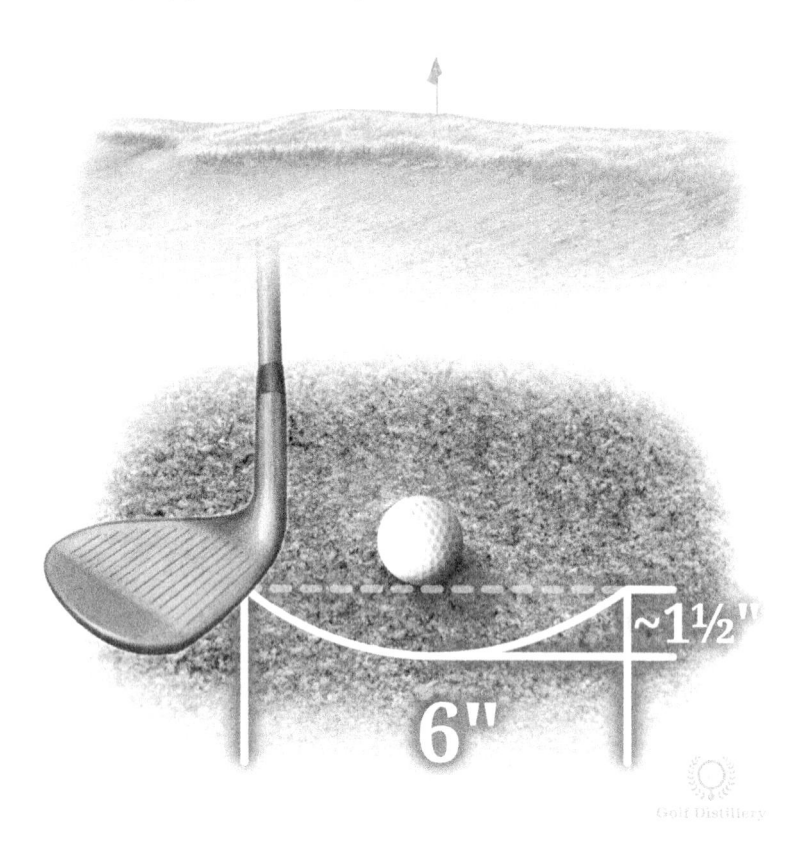

3.3 BUNKER SHOT DRILL

This bunker shot drill is very simple but very effective. I believe it to be the quickest way to improve your bunker play and build confidence in the sand.

But don't be put off by its simplicity. If you work with this drill you'll get a feel for splashing just the right amount of sand at just the right point.

- Draw a line in a practice bunker and set up so that it runs right through the centre of your stance.

- Make a swing aiming to take a divot in the sand that starts at the line and is about six inches in length, as we've just covered in the previous lesson.

- Move forward along the line making swings of various lengths. Some can be full swings but also include very short backswings where the clubhead stops at knee height. It's delicate bunker shots like these that cause most golfers to decelerate through impact.

- Remember your good bunker shot setup. The clubface should be completely open. Aim your feet and hips left (for the right-handed golfer) and remember to swing along the line of your feet — not towards the flag.

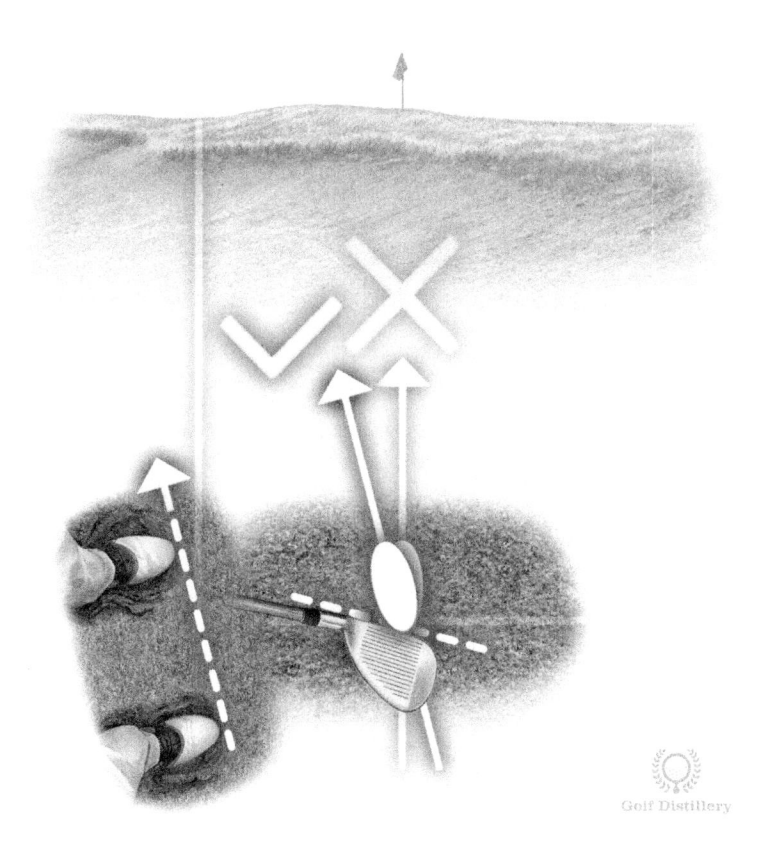

3.4 BUNKER SHOT DISTANCE CONTROL

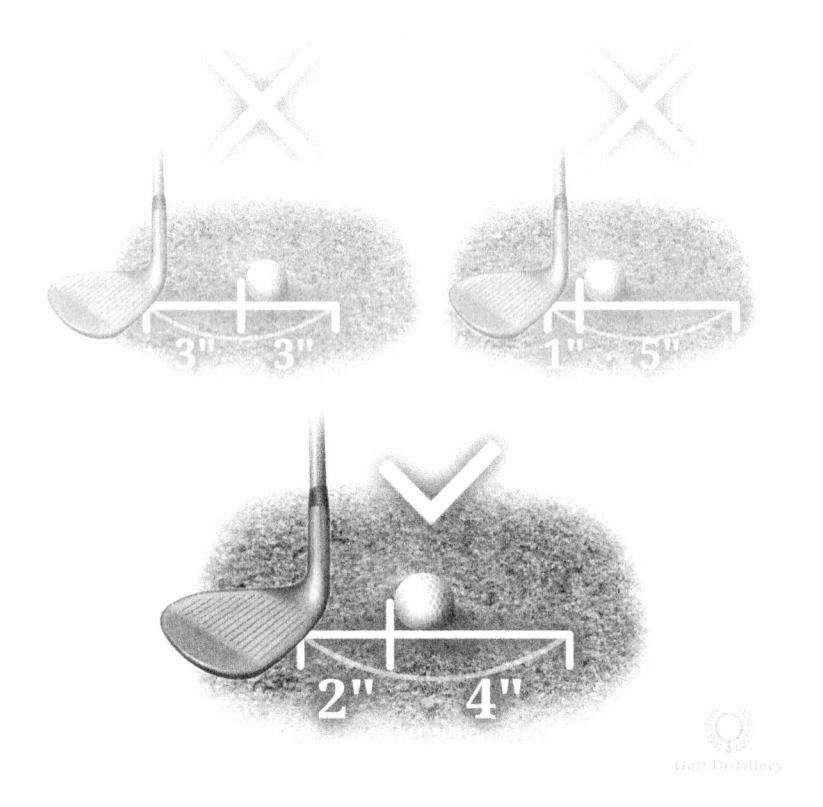

Many golfers are probably happy just to get the ball out of the bunker on their first try and landing it anywhere on the green.

But if you've spent even a relatively short amount of time practicing the previous bunker drill with a good bunker shot setup, you'll appreciate that golf shots out of the sand aren't particularly difficult.

You'll have a lot more confidence that you can get the ball close enough to the pin — wherever it is on the green — to give yourself a good chance of making the putt.

Essentially, there are two ways you can control your bunker shot distance.

You can either make the same-length swing each time while taking more or less sand. Or you can take the same amount of sand while shortening or lengthening your swing. I recommend the latter.

- It's much easier to control how the ball flies by taking the same amount of sand every time but varying your swing length.

- Most amateur golfers feel they have to take a full swing to ensure that the ball gets out of a bunker. But this is because they usually take too much sand. When you take the right amount of sand you can make short, controlled swings for those nearby, tricky pin positions.

- In order to avoid the common mistake of decelerating in your downswing make your follow through twice the length of your backswing. Your bunker shot swing should therefore consist of one-third backswing and two-thirds follow through.

3.5 BUNKER SHOTS FROM COMPACT OR WET SAND

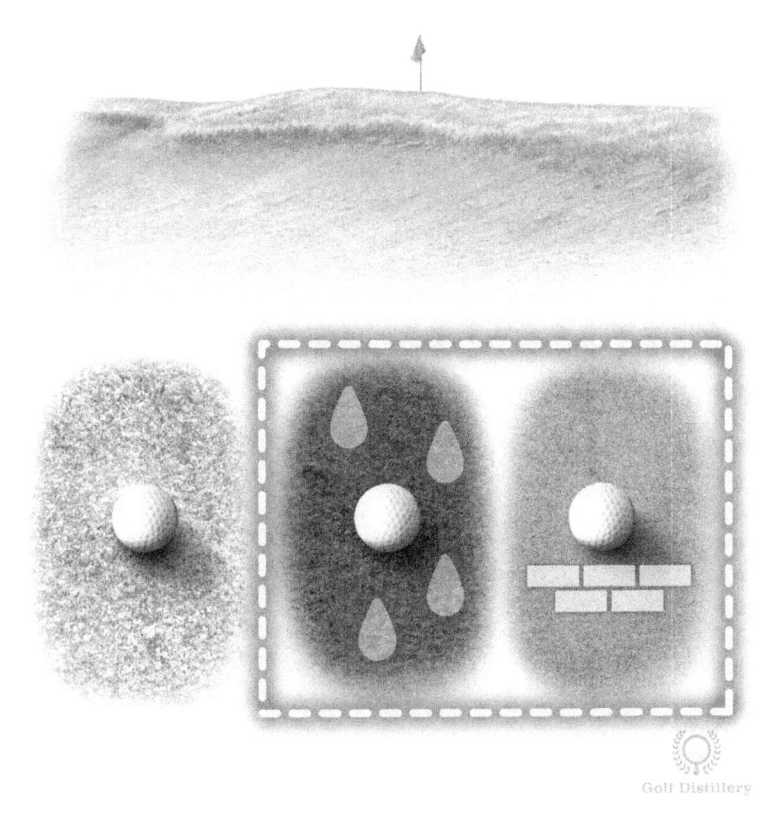

Once you're comfortable playing a basic bunker shot we can look at more troublesome sand play. The next few lessons will do just that.

I think it's fair to say that if most golfers don't like playing from the sand, they dread playing bunker shots from compacted, wet sand. That's because wet, compact or semi-frozen sand, or bunkers that don't have a lot of

3 - BUNKER SHOTS 117

sand in them often invite those destructive, thinned bunker shots.

Bunkers with wet sand are common here in the UK. But we're not the only country to get rain and except for the very best golf courses, the greenskeeper staff won't have the time to always keep bunkers in a perfectly raked condition.

There are certain adjustments you can make to both your setup and club selection to get a good contact out of wet sand and give yourself a chance of getting up and down.

- Normally, we'd always opt for a sand wedge out of a greenside bunker [1] because the additional bounce prevents the club from digging into the sand. From wet [2] or compacted sand [3] however, a lob wedge with about 60 degrees of loft is more suitable. This will allow the club to cut through the sand where a sand wedge is more likely to bounce off the top.

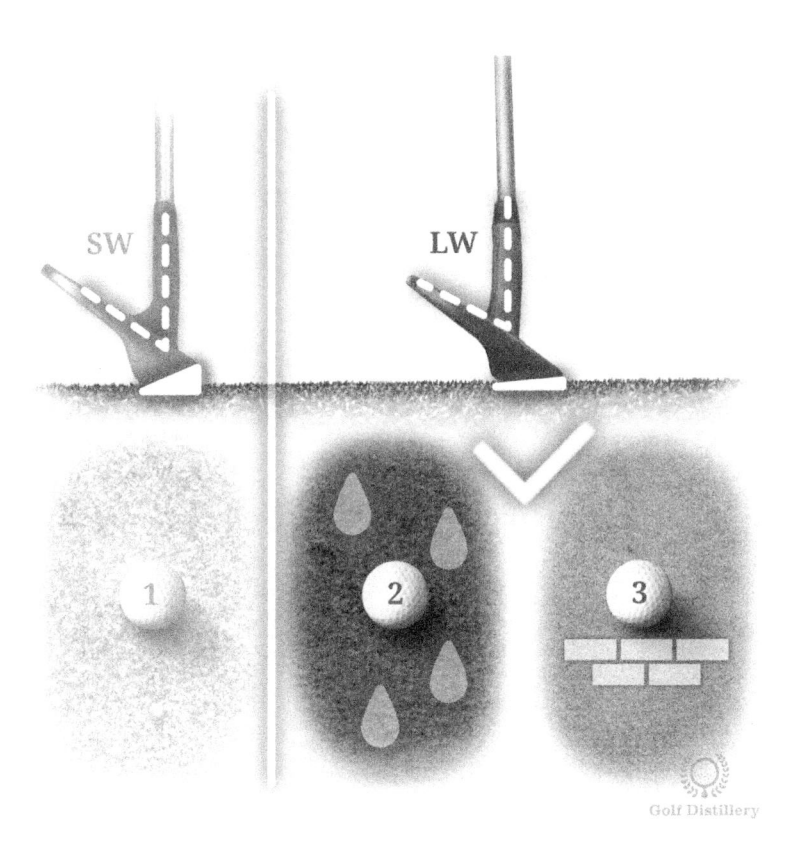

- While we would normally take two inches of sand behind the ball, aim to strike the sand only one inch behind the ball in wet or hard conditions. More than that and the club will slow down too quickly, causing a very heavy shot that might leave the ball in the bunker.

- Set up as normal with a nice wide stance, feet firmly planted and ball slightly ahead of centre. Grip down for control, feet aiming left of target to compensate for the open clubface aiming well right.

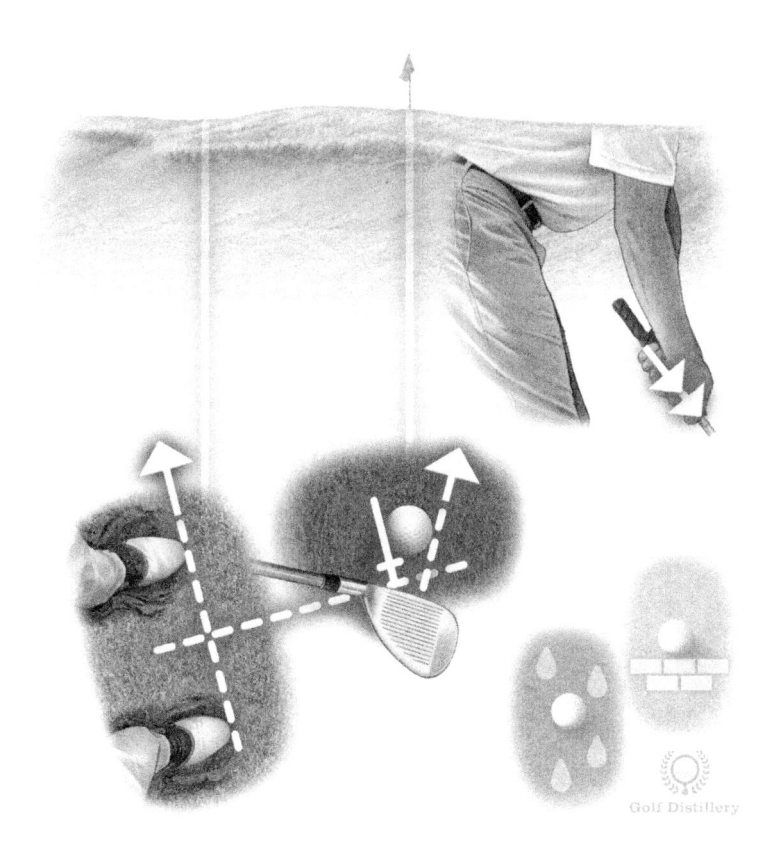

- Aim to skim the sand instead of digging a deeper divot. Trust that the sharper leading edge of the lob wedge will cut through the sand rather than bounce off it.

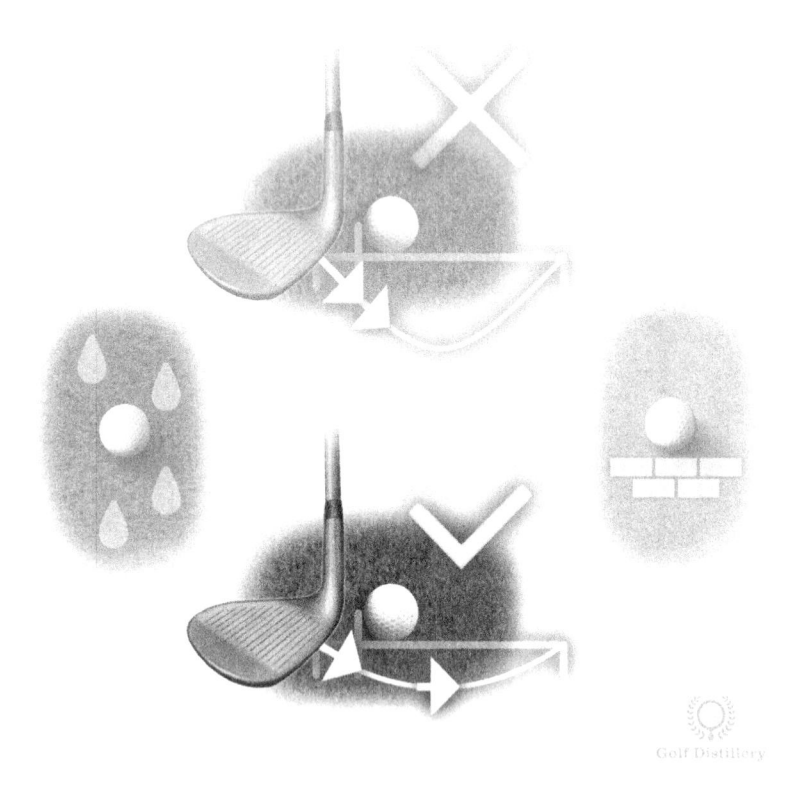

3.6 BUNKER SHOTS FROM A PLUGGED LIE

Bunker shots from a plugged lie are perceived as one of the toughest shots in golf. But they need not be.

For the uninitiated, a plugged lie is when the ball sits half-buried (or more) in the sand. This can happen if the ball flies straight into the bunker from quite a long, high shot. Or it can happen after rolling into a natural crater in the sand.

Either way, we need to adjust our setup and the way we play bunker shots from a plugged lie compared to normal sand play.

- Normally, we'd aim to strike the sand two inches behind the ball and exit our divot four inches after the ball. But for a plugged lie I'd like you to imagine a box around the ball that is about three inches from the ball on all sides. The aim is to remove this entire box of sand.

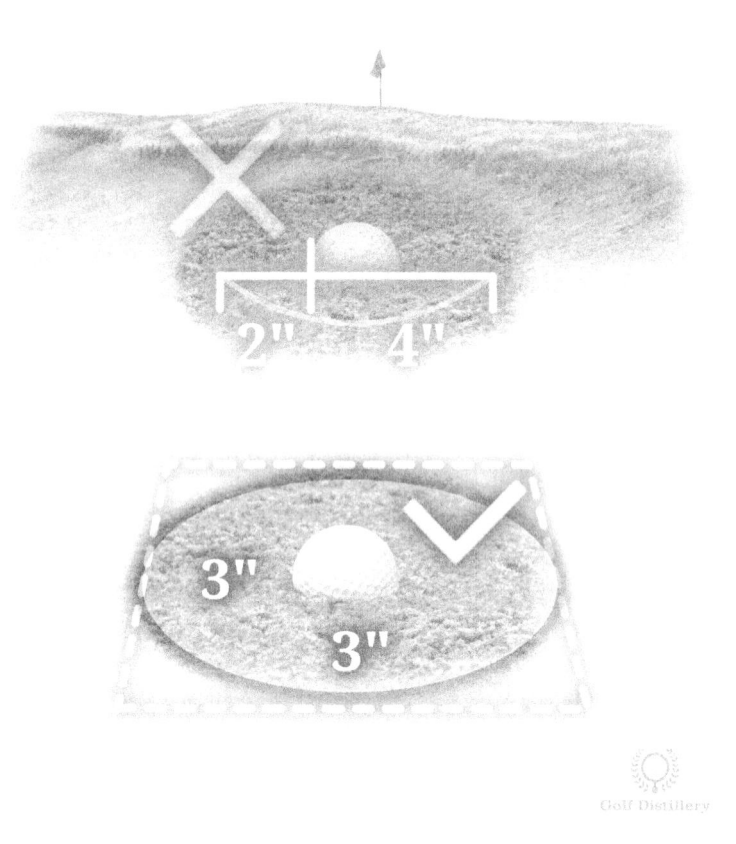

- Use a sand wedge as the extra bounce will prevent the club from digging too much into the sand, which would cause you to hit the shot too heavy.

- The setup is similar to a normal bunker shot with shoulder-width stance, feet dug in for balance, ball played ahead of centre in the stance. The clubhead will enter the sand at a point that corresponds to the dead centre of your stance.

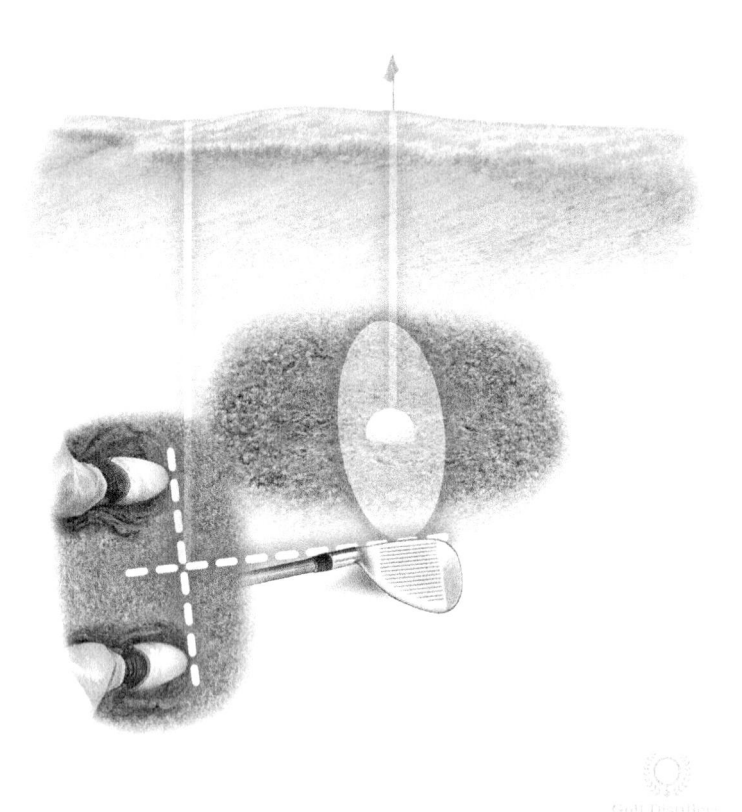

- Keep the clubface square — not open like with standard bunker shots. As a result, also remember to align your feet and hips only slightly left of target, shoulders square to the target.

- Grip down the club for control but here we want to grip really tightly, with a grip pressure of 9 out of 10. This will help prevent the club from twisting and decelerating quickly as it goes deeply into the sand.

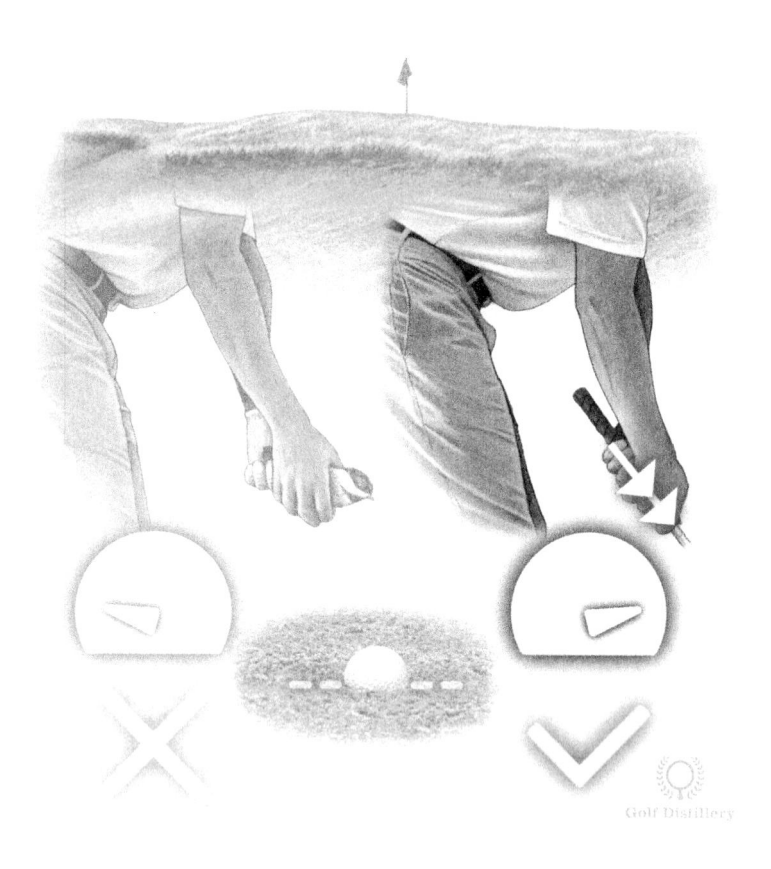

- Really emphasize the follow through so that you drive as much sand forward on to the green as possible.

- Remember, there will be very little spin on the golf ball and you might have to accept the ball rolling past the pin. Don't get too cute trying to finish pin high as you need to be very aggressive to get the ball out of its plugged lie.

3.7 BUNKER SHOTS FROM SLOPING LIES

In this lesson we'll tackle how to play a bunker shot where the ball is sitting on a sloping lie.

You'll actually come across a sloping lie in the bunker more often than you might think as the ball can easily roll up towards the lip and leave you an uphill or downhill lie.

Here's how to play them.

– UPHILL SLOPE (UPSLOPE)

- On an uphill slope the ball is going to come out quite steeply which will help us stop it quickly on the green.

- Playing from an upslope in a fairway bunker we would usually take a less-lofted club to try to lower an otherwise high ball flight. However, on an upslope from a greenside bunker you'll probably have a bunker lip very close by to clear. So opt for your lofted sand wedge, as normal.

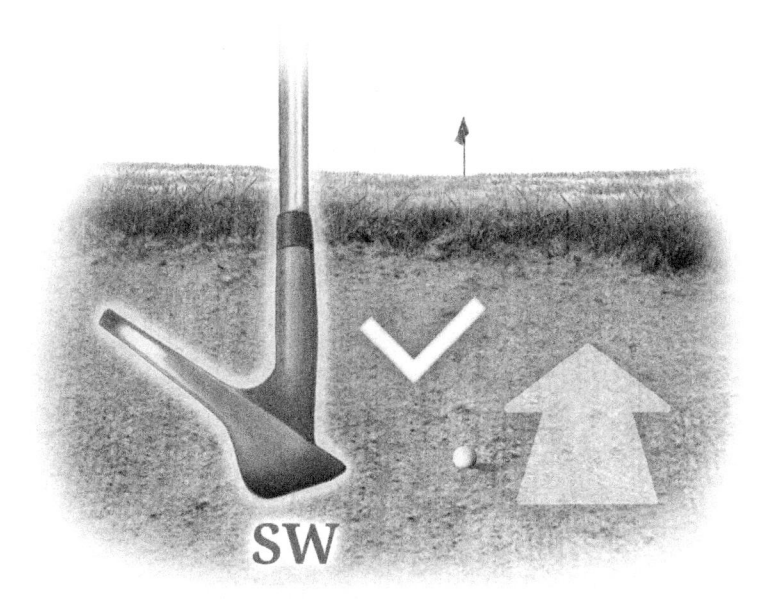

- As you address the ball take a much wider stance to anchor yourself into the hill. Tilt your shoulders back so they are aligned with the slope and keep the clubface open as you would normally.

- Keep your legs very still. There should be little or no leg movement for the duration of the swing.

- Strike the sand about two inches behind the golf ball as normal, with the ball slightly ahead of centre in your stance.

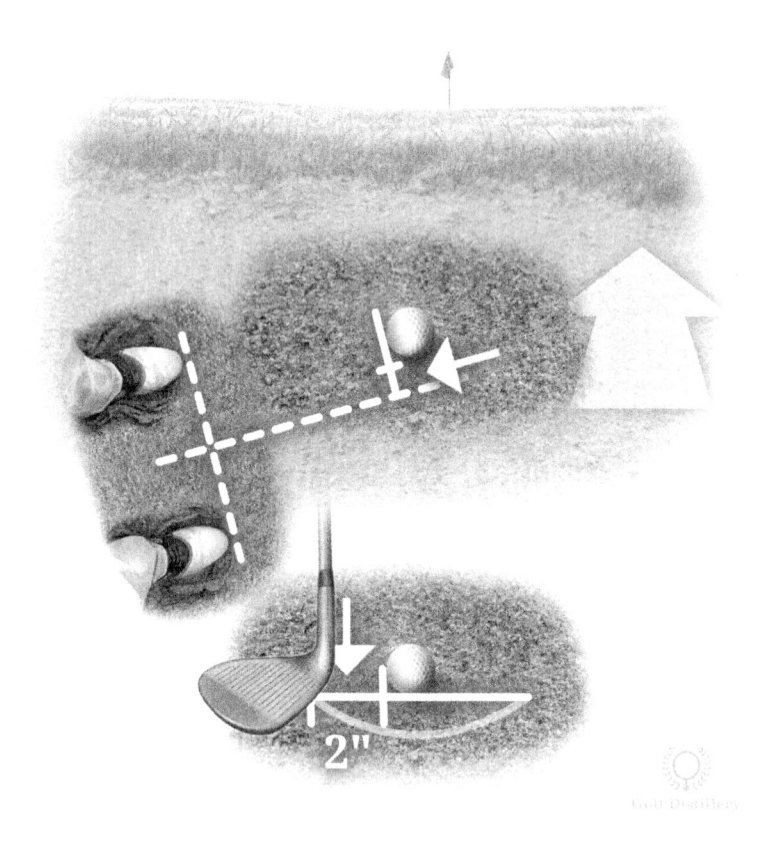

- As you strike through the ball allow the club to 'chase up' the slope. We want to avoid the club digging into the sand bank. Instead, allow the club to travel up the slope to give the shot its height.

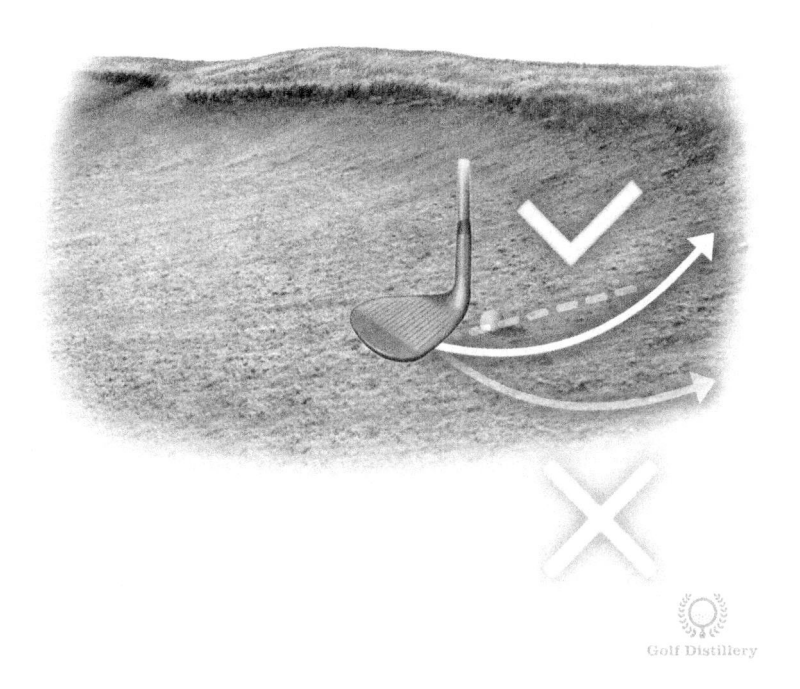

- You'll need to hit the shot with enough power to land the ball close to the flag. The high ball flight associated with this shot means you'll get very little roll.

– DOWNHILL SLOPE (DOWNSLOPE)

- On a downhill slope the ball is going to fly out at a shallower-than-normal angle. This will also give it more roll.

- Open the clubface as much as possible. You may also want to use a 60-degree lob wedge over your sand wedge here.

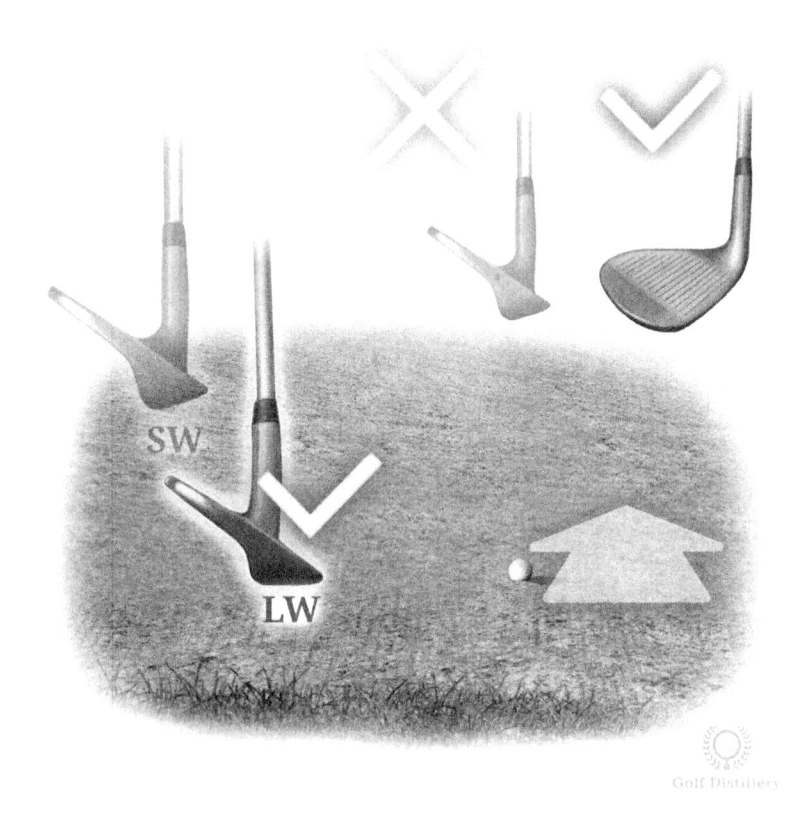

- To minimize the effect of the slope tilt your shoulders down along the line of the slope. The bodyweight will lean a bit more into the left side as well (for the right-handed golfer).

- Similarly to the upslope bunker shot take a much wider stance to retain good balance through the shot.

- Keep your legs very still. There should be little or no leg movement for the duration of the swing.

- Strike the sand about two inches behind the golf ball as normal, with the ball slightly ahead of centre in your stance.

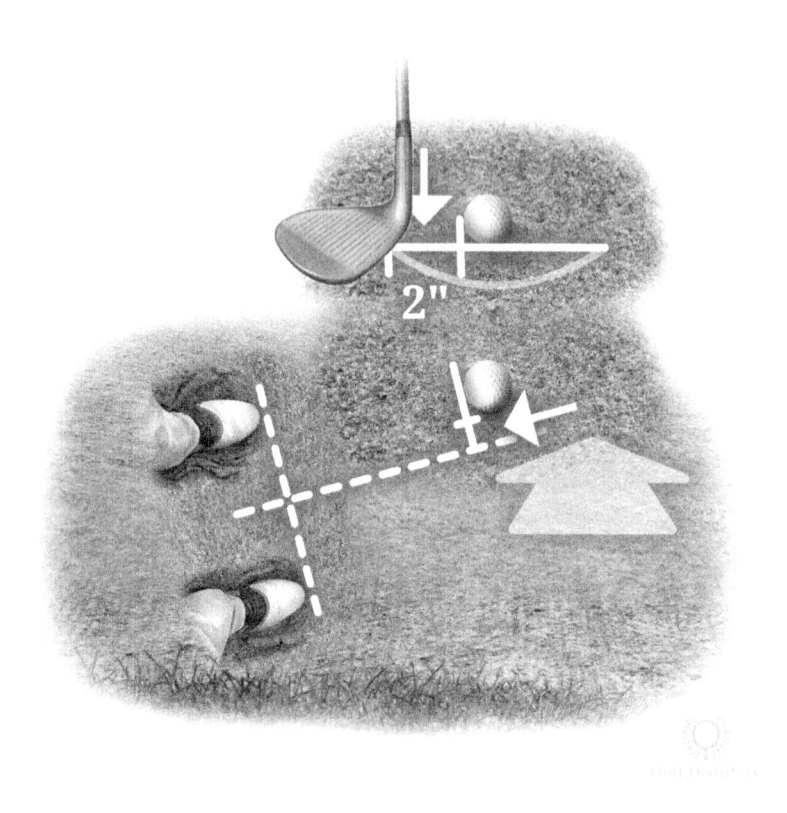

- As you strike through the ball, feel as though the clubhead is 'chasing down' the slope. This will help to minimize the chance of catching the ball thin.

- Accept that from a downhill sloping lie, anything out of the bunker in one stroke and anywhere on the green is a good result.

3.8 FAIRWAY BUNKER SHOTS

In this last lesson before moving on to putting we'll look at some key tips for playing fairway bunker shots.

Fairway bunkers tend to be a bit bigger and flatter than greenside bunkers, giving you an opportunity to take a less lofted club than the sand wedge and getting the golf ball further up towards the green.

That being said, the cardinal sin is getting too greedy — hitting the bunker lip and leaving the ball in the sand.

I'll teach you a useful tip for gauging whether a certain club can launch the ball high enough, quickly enough to avoid catching the lip. I also cover the basic setup and swing technique you'll want to adopt for fairway bunker shots.

- To judge whether a particular club can clear the lip of a bunker place the clubhead on the ground and gently step on the clubface so that the back of the clubhead is flush with the ground. The clubface should point towards the sky, under your foot.

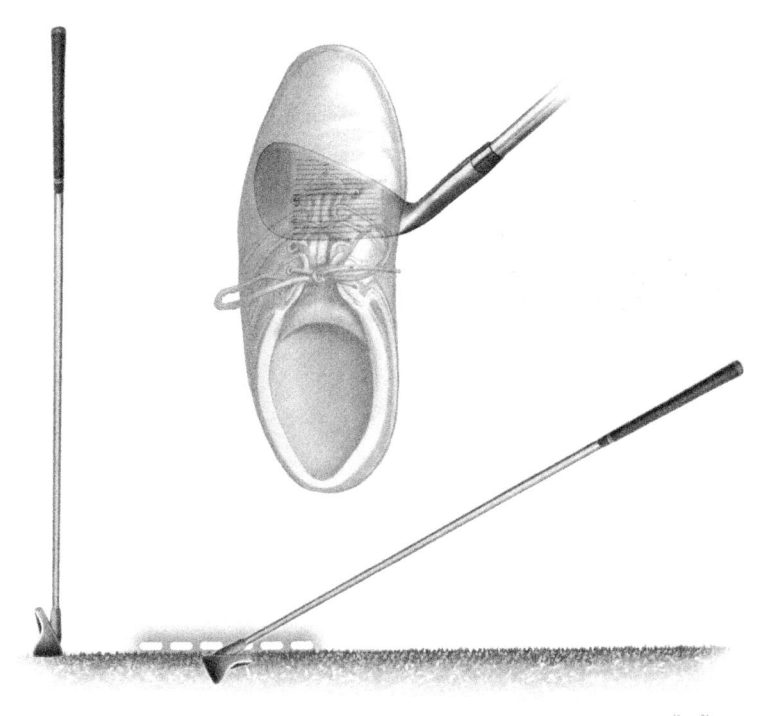

- The angle that the club shaft makes against the ground more or less matches the trajectory of the ball flight. Obviously you need to do this at the side of the fairway bunker as touching the sand with your club will result in a penalty.

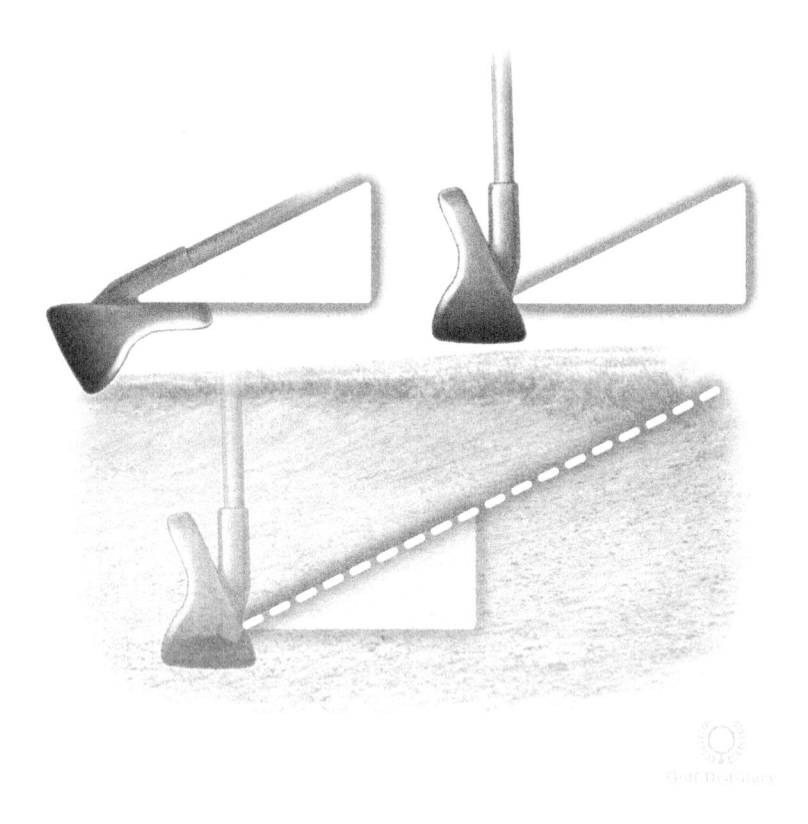

- Whatever club you think you can get away with, add one just to be safe. So if you think a 7-iron will clear the lip take an 8-iron instead.

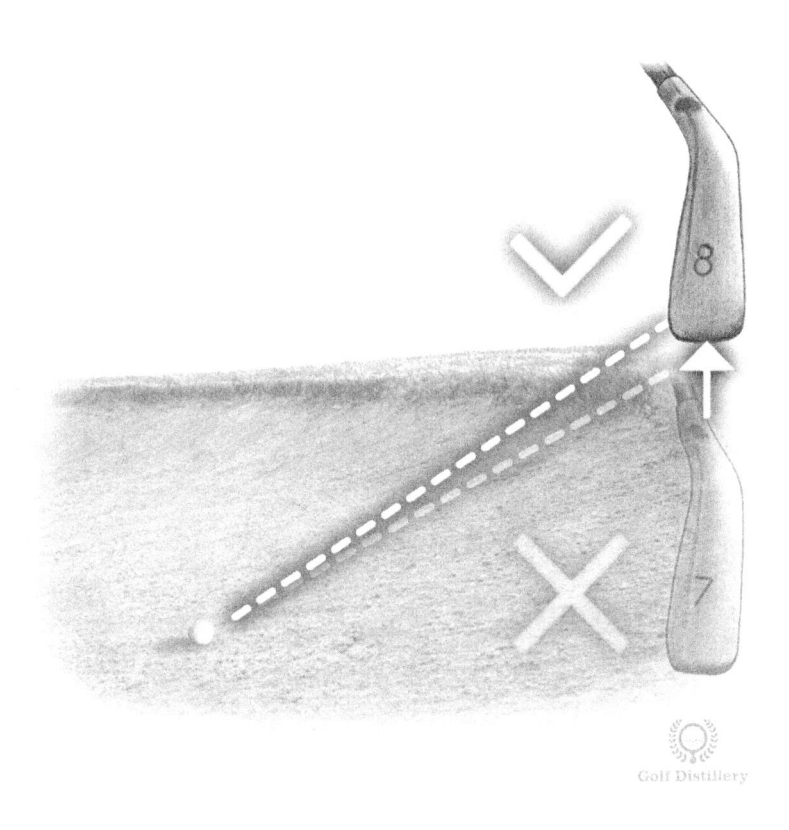

- Setting up, take a standard address position but move the ball back slightly to about the centre of your stance. That will encourage a cleaner contact.

- Unlike from a greenside bunker shot we don't want to hit the sand first here. Instead, your aim is to hit the ball and then take a divot of sand.

- During your downswing make a good move to your left side through impact (for the right-handed golfer). There can be a tendency to stay back on the right foot, leading to a thin or fat mishit.

- Finally, increase your grip pressure more than usual as this will help to prevent the sand twisting the club and slowing it down too much.

4 - PUTTING

In the last section of this short game guide we'll focus on what I truly believe is the most important club in the golf bag — the putter.

The following lessons cover all aspects of good putting fundamentals in alignment, stance and ball position, posture, grip, stroke, and distance control. But I also cover how to read greens and how to putt using a hybrid club from off the green.

Finally, I conclude this section (and guide) with a drill to help you gain confidence with short putts.

Why is Putting so Important?

I don't think most golfers appreciate just how many shots they are throwing away with their putter. If you want to lower your scores and your handicap as quickly as possible, improve your putting.

The following will help you appreciate just how many putts you could be wasting.

- Count the number of putts you take per round over an average of three rounds.
- If you're taking more than 36 putts per round — which would be more than the average of two

putts per hole — you're wasting shots on the golf course.
- If, like many higher handicappers you're taking 40+ putts per round, it's like you are taking half a dozen whiffs on the first tee. You wouldn't do that too often before doing something about it, would you?
- There's no reason why any level of golfer can't become a very good putter with proper instruction and a bit of practice.
- Unlike the physically demanding full golf swing, putting is a skill that can be mastered regardless of age or physical strength.

4.1 PUTTING ALIGNMENT

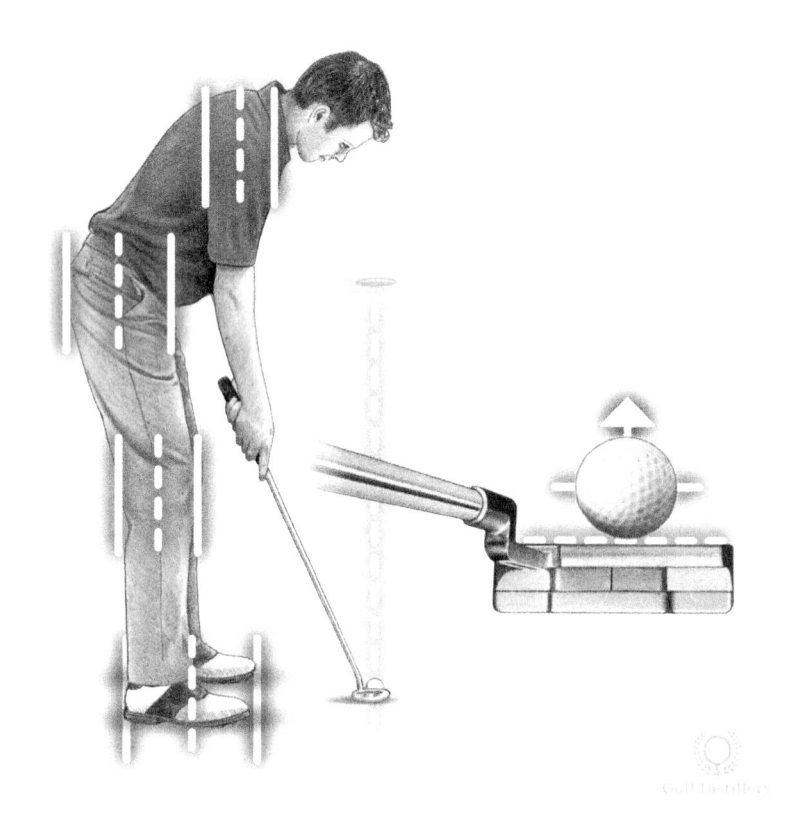

In this first lesson we'll start by looking at putting alignment.

As with the full golf swing, alignment is something that appears so obvious and so simple that we forget to check it on a regular basis.

Remind yourself to pay close attention to the alignment

of your feet, your hips and your shoulders, especially when you practice on the putting green.

I'd also encourage you to incorporate an 'alignment check' into your pre-shot routine.

- Start by aiming the putter face at your initial target, which is not necessarily the hole because there could be some break to allow for. Then build your stance around the putter's position. This is in contrast to trying to line your stance up first and then aiming the putter face.

- The line of your feet should aim parallel left of the target (for the right-handed golfer). That means the ball-to-target line and the line of your feet are perfectly parallel.

- Alignment is not just about your feet. Your feet act as a line for your knees, hips and shoulders to follow. Pay particular attention to the line of your shoulders.

4.2 PUTTING STANCE & BALL POSITION

After checking for good alignment the next fundamental is the putting stance.

Specifically, we'll look at the width of your stance, the ball position in the stance and the position of the hands.

I also make a reference to the length of your putter. I see many club golfers that have putters that are too long for them. It's an easy job for your local PGA professional to shorten your putter so if possible I'd encourage you to get fitted for the length of your putter shaft.

- The width of your stance should be roughly hip-width with the feet pointing forward — not splayed out.

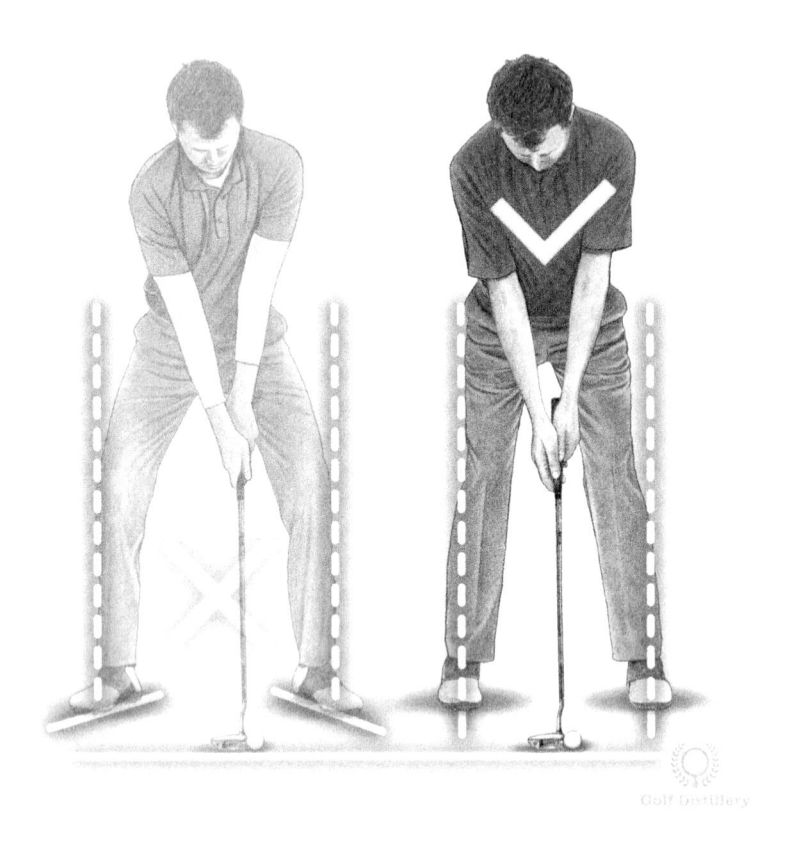

- The ball should be positioned slightly ahead of the centre of your stance, similarly to its position were you to address it with a 6-iron.

- As you rest the putter on the ground, position your hands so that the grip of the putter points towards your left hip, just left of your belt buckle (for the right-handed golfer). Your hands should be slightly ahead of the golf ball.

- This slight 'forward press' is something that is missing in the setup of many amateur golfers. It de-lofts the putter face, improving the roll of the ball and the overall quality of the putt.

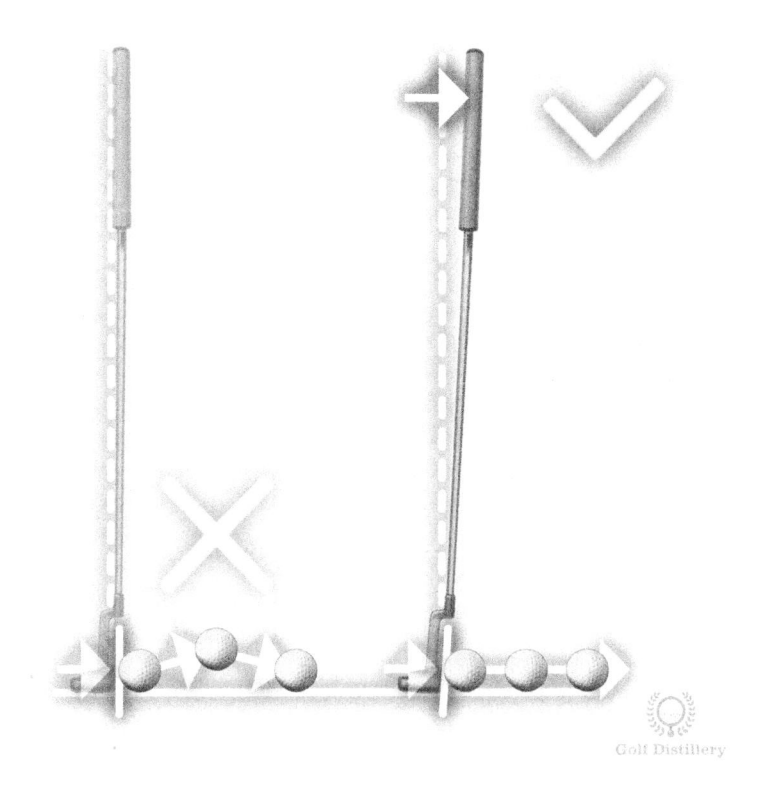

- Many golfers have putters that are too long for them. Your hands and arms should hang down in a relaxed, neutral position. Grip the putter where your hands fall even if it means holding the club right at the bottom of the grip. You could even consider getting your putter shaft shortened.

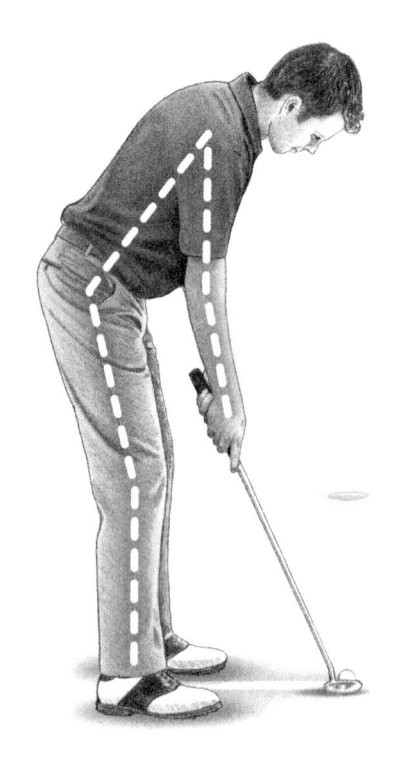

4.3 PUTTING POSTURE

In the previous two lessons we looked at the alignment, stance, ball and hand positions of the putting setup.

Another checkpoint that could improve your putting is your posture or the position of your head over the golf ball and in particular, the position of your eyes.

As you might guess, your eyes should be positioned directly over the golf ball. If they are not it really does compromise your ability to see the line of the putt. Most golfers will feel that this is the position they take because they are always looking directly at the ball. However, the following quick test might tell you otherwise.

- A great way to check if your eyes are directly over the ball is to first set up to a putt as normal. Then, hold another golf ball in your left eye socket (for the right-handed golfer) and let it drop. It should hit the ball on the ground.

- With a full swing setup your head would be held in a position that runs mostly in line with the angle of your spine — you feel as though you are looking down your nose at the ball. To improve your putting, let your head drop so that when you turn your head to look at the hole, your line of sight runs right up and down the target line.

4.4 PUTTING GRIP

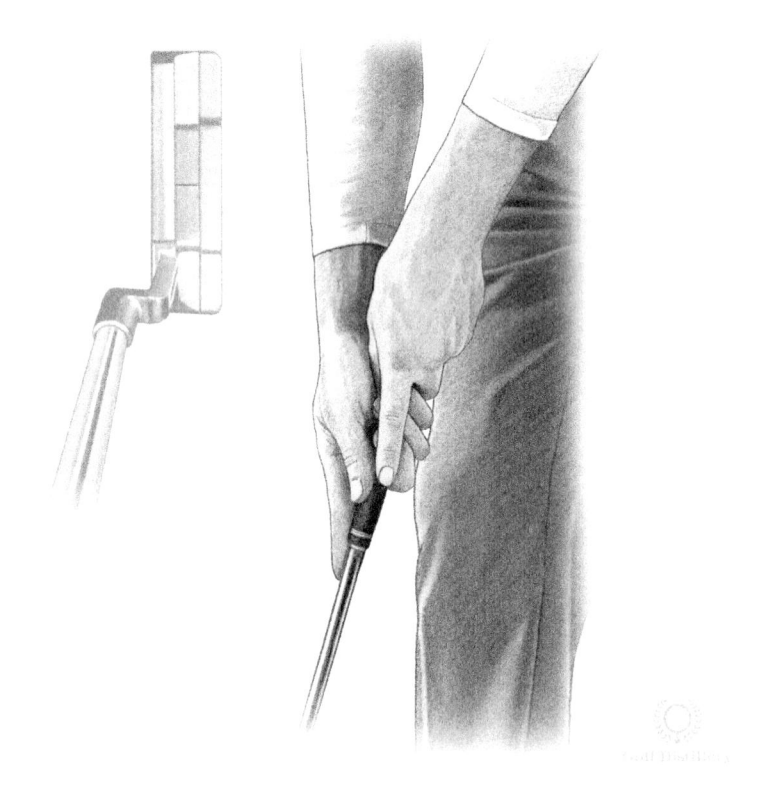

The final component of a good putting setup is holding the putter correctly in your hands.

A full swing grip is designed to allow and promote quite a lot of wrist hinge — an important part of generating power. But when we're putting we don't want any wrist hinge at all. Instead, we'd like to keep the wrists as solid as possible.

The following lesson features a step-by-step guide to a good, standard putting grip.

Now, there are variations on this putting grip and many of them are even used by the top Tour players. We'll review a few of those in section 4.7.

But if you're just getting started, try the standard putting grip first and then experiment with gripping the putter in some alternative ways to see if those suit you better.

- Begin by gripping the putter in the same way you would any of your other clubs. This should place your left and right hands in a neutral position on the club.

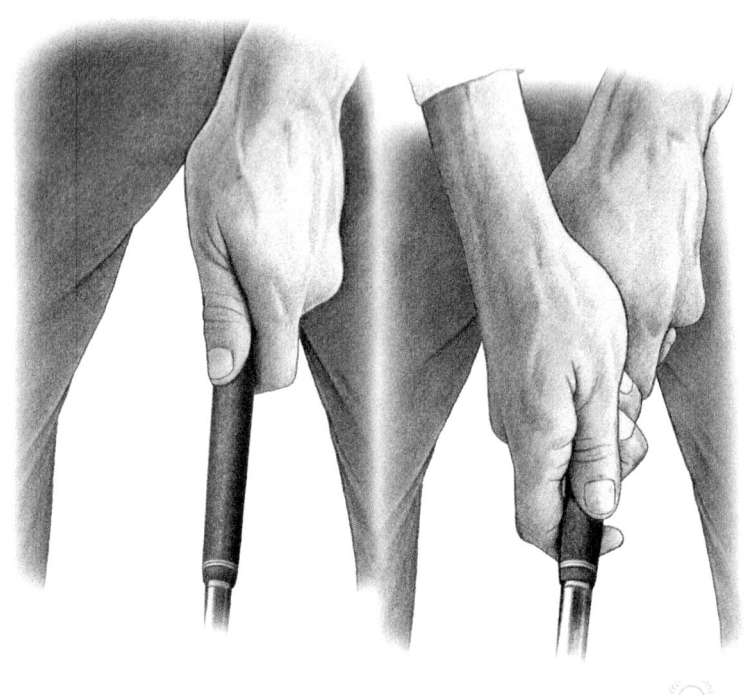

- Next, unlink your little fingers at the back so your hands sit on top of each other like they would in a baseball grip.

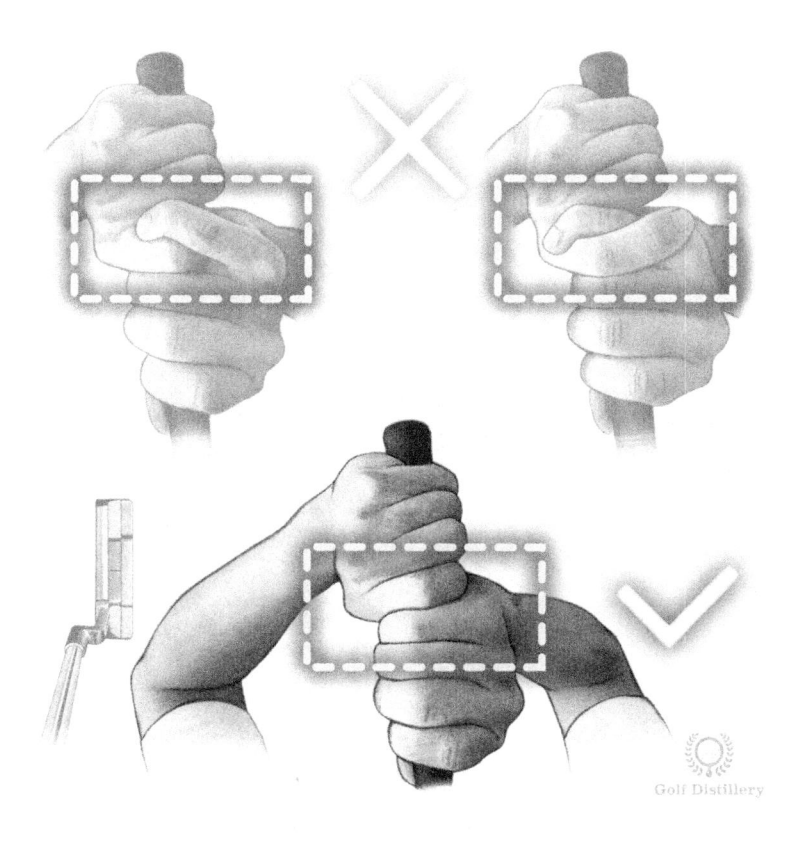

- Now take your right index finger (for the right-handed golfer) and place it down the shaft of the club. Then, 'unpeel' your left index finger and run that one over the fingernails of your right hand, pointing down the shaft of the club.

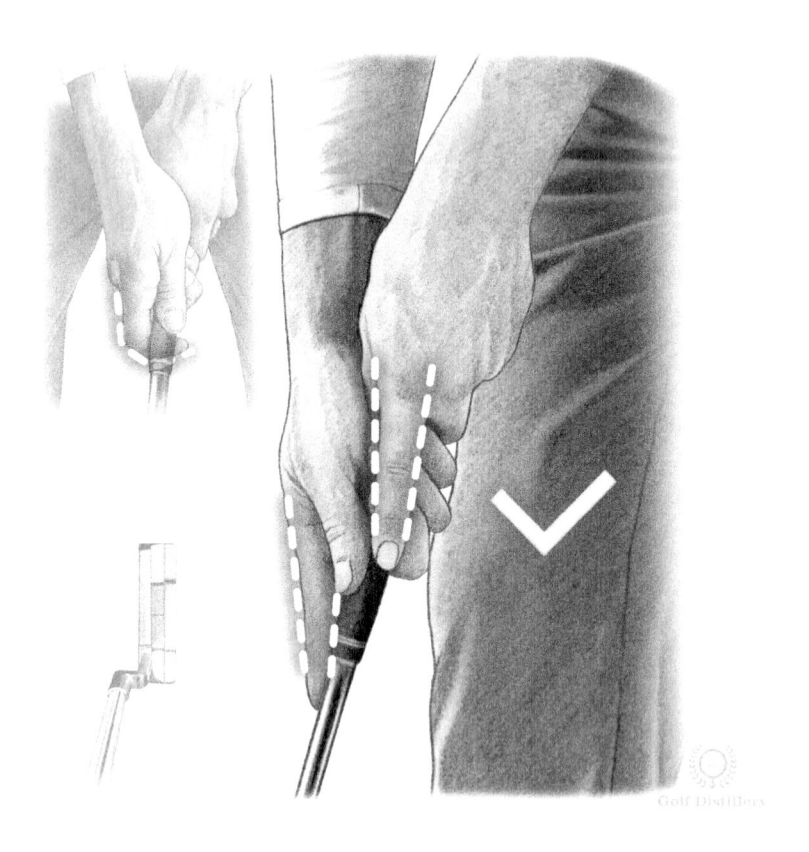

- In effect, your index fingers work as mini splints to prevent wrist break.

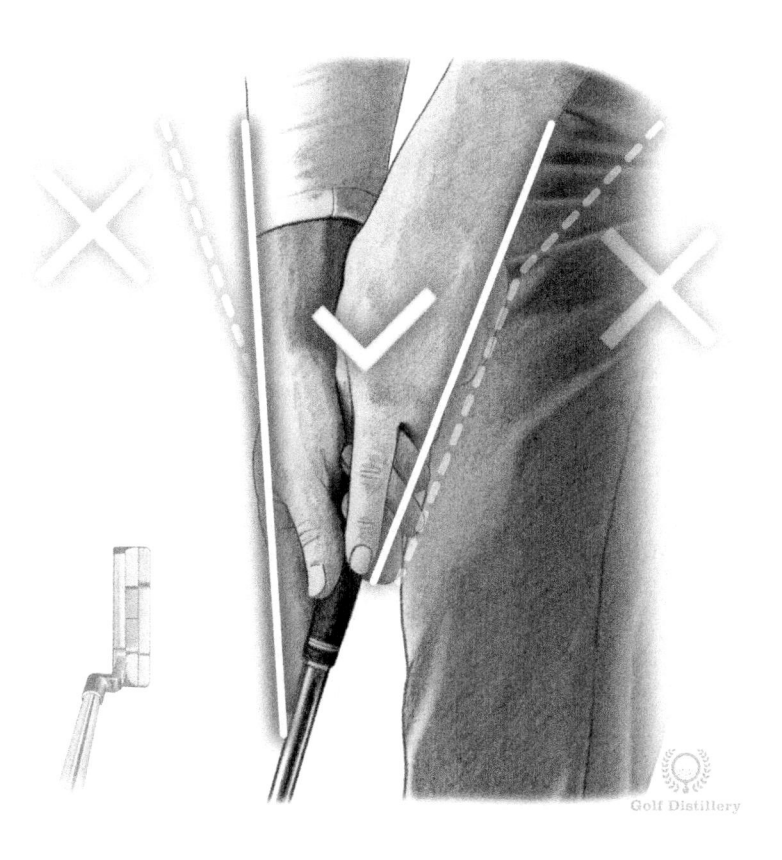

- You may want to try a few alternative putting grips after you've given this standard grip a try. If so, refer to section 4.7 for more on these.

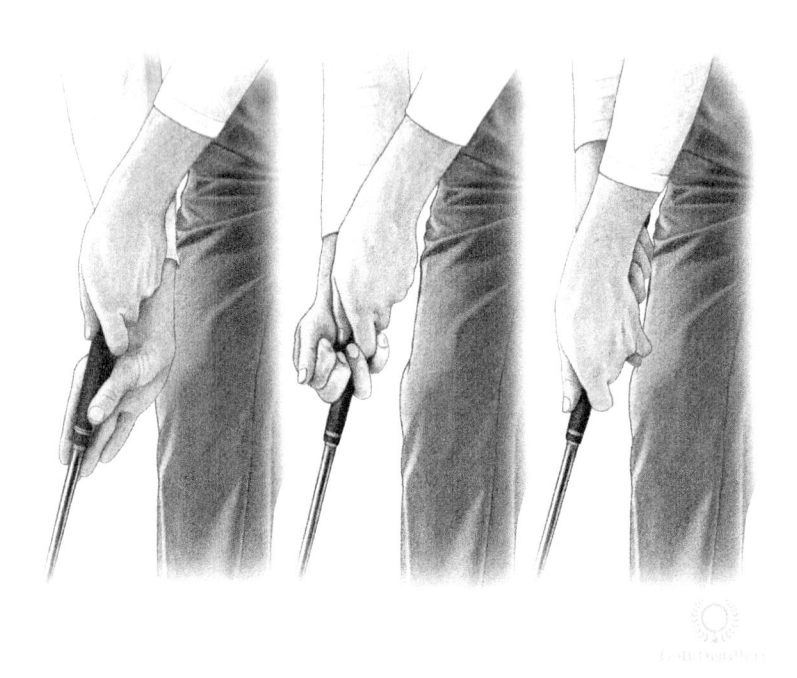

4.5 PUTTING STROKE

In this penultimate fundamentals lesson we'll look at the putting stroke itself.

A good putting stroke has few moving parts and is anchored around a single rhythm — or cadence, regardless of the length of putt. That way you can simply make a longer or shorter stroke to vary the lengths of your putts with both accuracy and consistency.

After this lesson we'll look in more detail at how you can control the distance of your putts. But you can't begin to master distance control until you have a reliable, repeatable putting stroke.

- The putting stroke should be dominated by the shoulders. A rocking of the shoulders moves the arms and hands together in one unit while keeping the wrists solid.

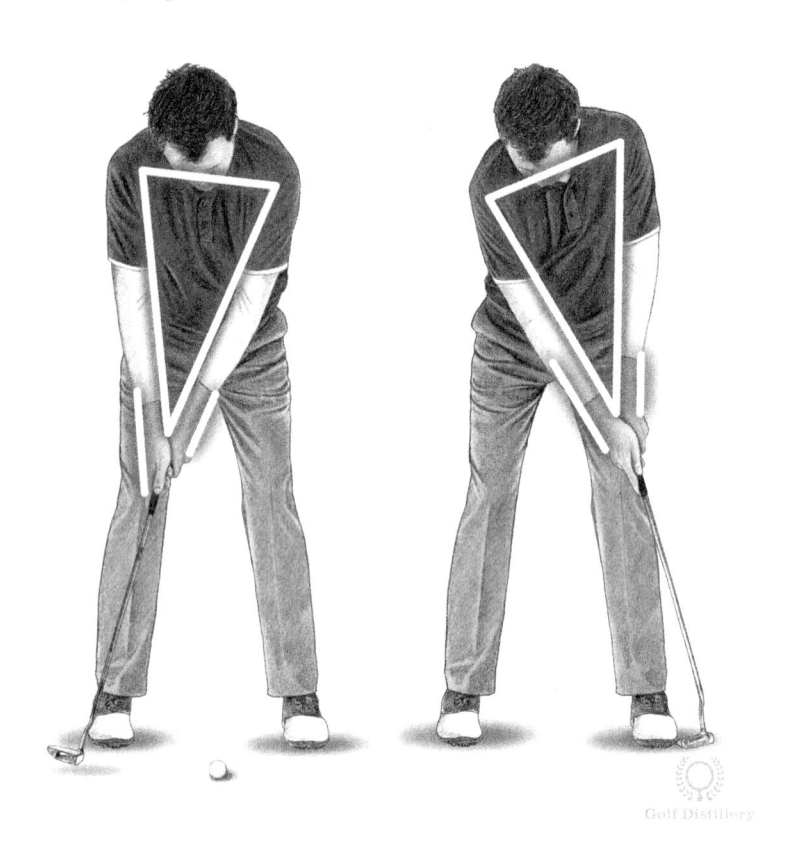

- Your lower half — hips, legs and feet — should stay completely still throughout the putting stroke. Your weight should remain split 50/50 across your two feet during the entire movement.

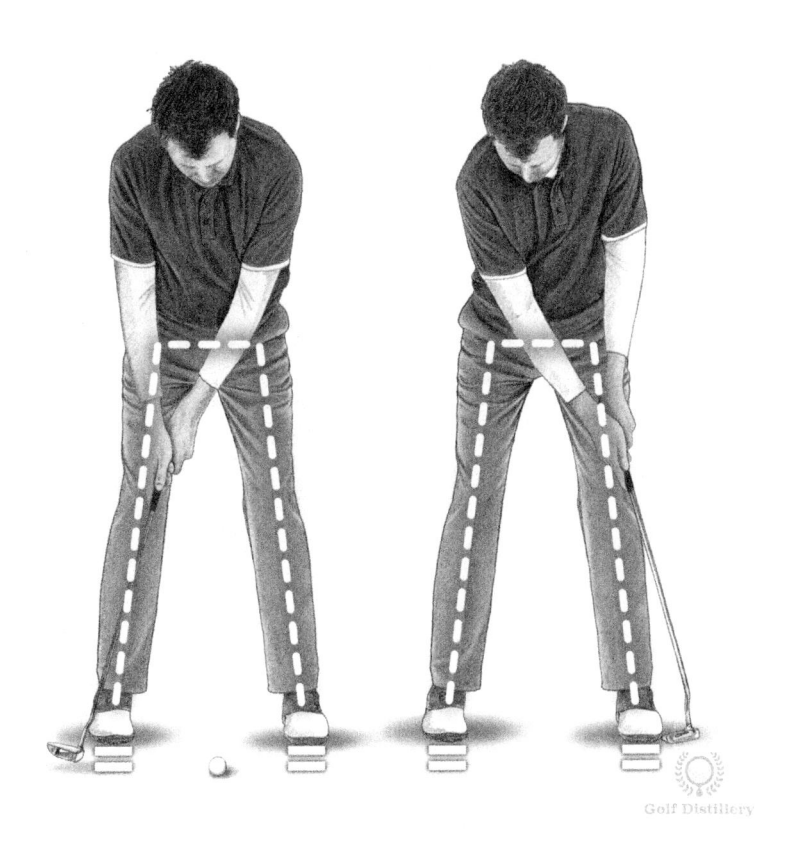

- The length of your backswing should closely match the length of your follow through.

- The rhythm of your putting stroke should always stay the same. You'd have the same rhythm for short 3-foot putts as you would for long 30-foot ones. The length of your putting stroke — not its speed — will determine the distance you hit each putt.

- The putter head should travel in a straight line back and a straight line through to the target.

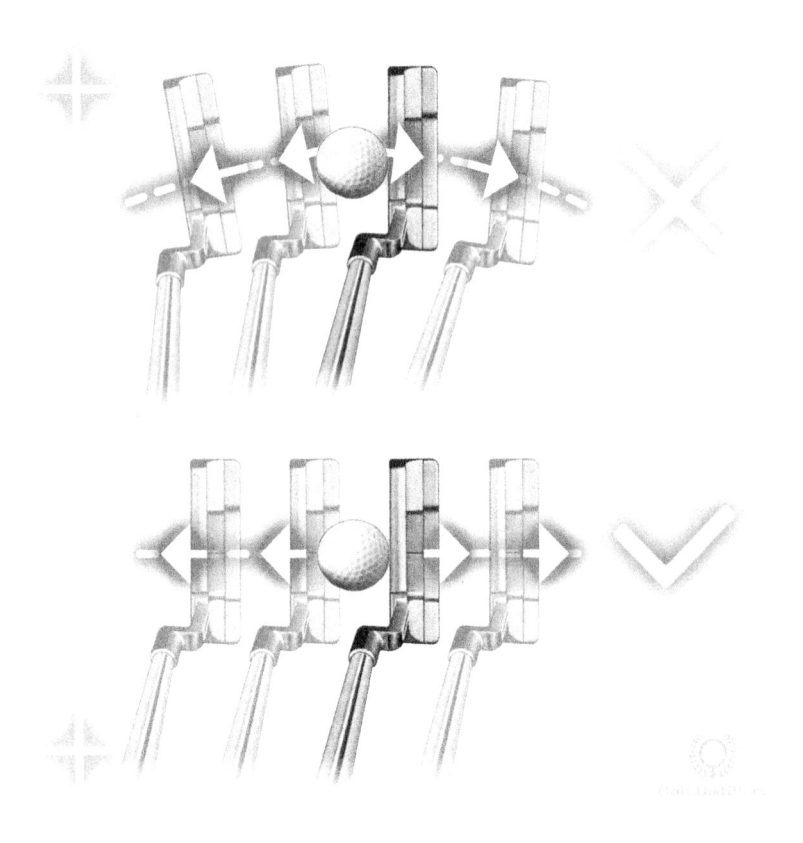

- Focus on keeping the putter face perfectly square — at right angles — to your target line as you make your stroke.

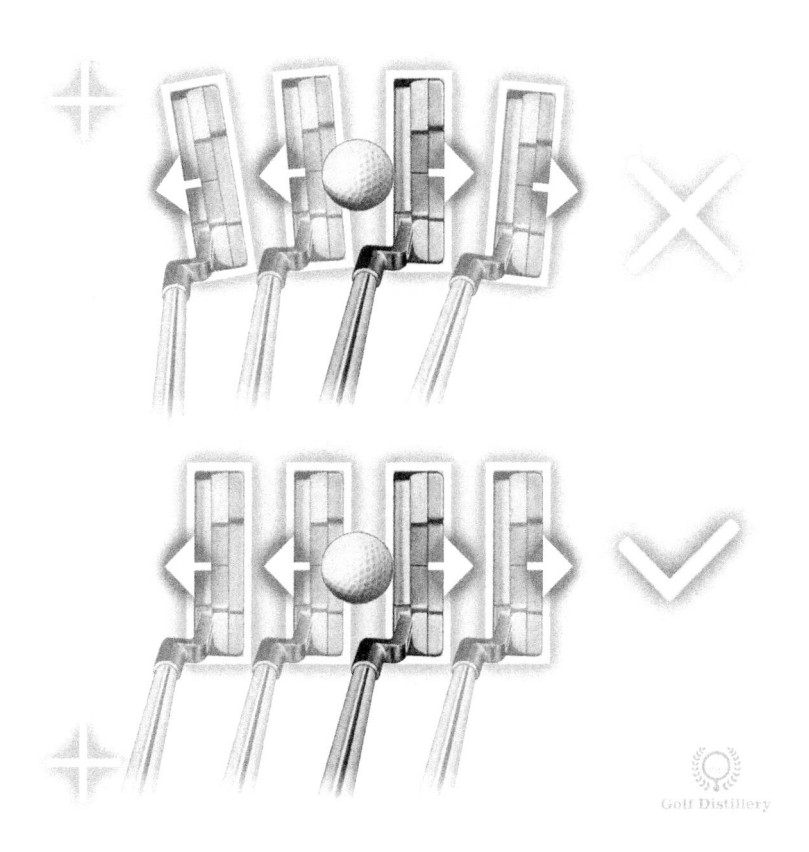

4.6 PUTTING DISTANCE CONTROL

If you can improve your putting distance control you'll drop handfuls of shots each round you play.

Just remember that your ability to gauge the distance of long putts — rather than your ability to accurately read the line of those putts — is what will likely eliminate those nasty 3-putts from your game.

For example, a golfer might have a 30 or 40-foot putt and they'll spend most of their pre-putting routine trying to figure out the various breaks in the green and the line the ball will take. They'll hit their putt and it might glance the hole but finish a good 10 feet past. "Unlucky", "Great effort" their playing partners might say. But chances are the return putt will be missed as well.

If you can focus instead on the appropriate weight of your putts and get the line roughly correct you'll rarely end up more than three feet away from the hole.

- First and foremost, appreciate the relative importance of distance control [A] over reading the line in long putts [B]. Get the distance right and you'll probably 2-putt at worst.

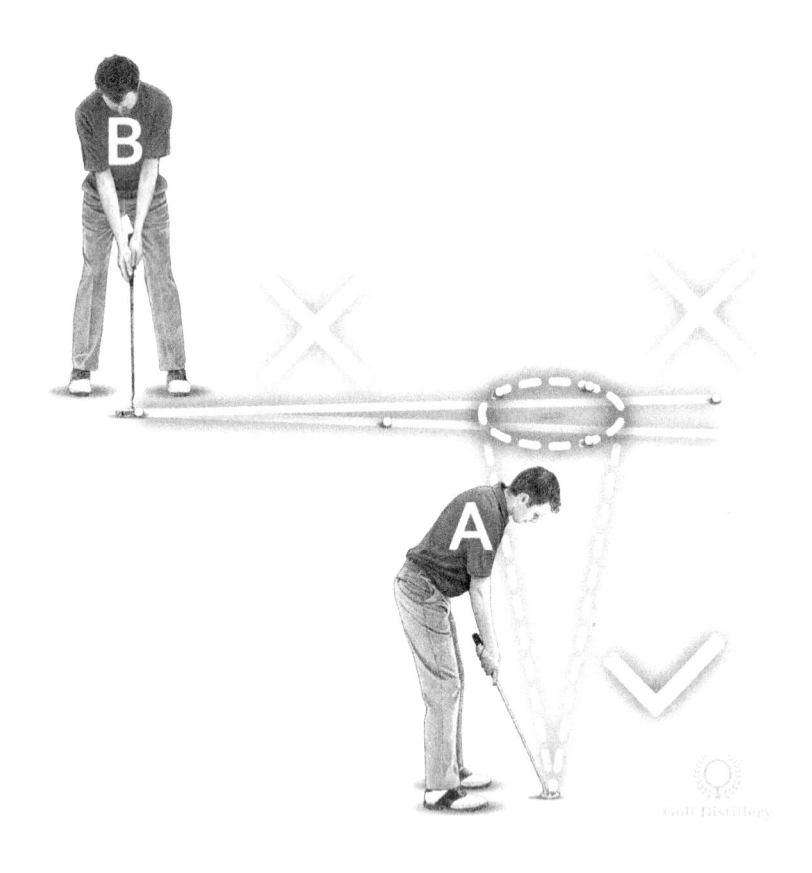

- Most golfers are fairly solid within three feet of the hole so ideally aim 18 inches past the hole. That gives the putt a chance to drop if you happen to get the line right. As you go through your pre-shot routine and setup keep your focus on a point 18 inches beyond the hole.

- Make a series of practice strokes, rocking the putter back and forth whilst looking at your target rather than down at the ball or at your putter head. Really feel as though you are hitting imaginary putts to your target and whether your length of practice stroke is too short, too long, or just about right.

- To help you with this 'feel' you can make some overly short practice strokes and some overly long ones as you're looking at the hole. You could then judge that something in between won't be too far off.

4.7 ALTERNATIVE PUTTING GRIP STYLES

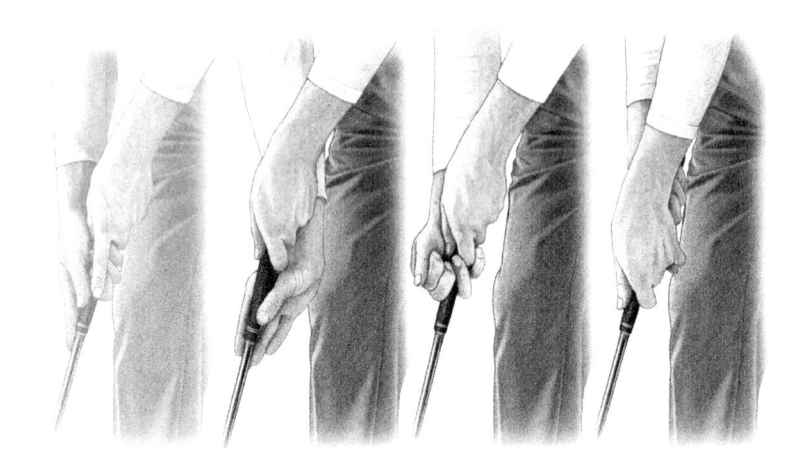

If you've watched golf over the years you'll know that the top golfers seem to use all manner of different putting grips.

In this lesson we'll highlight three alternative putting grips that are popular on Tour that you may want to experiment with. But before you do however, I recommend you familiarize yourself with the basic putting grip first (as seen in section 4.4).

- **Pencil Grip (or Pen Grip)**: The right hand (for the right-handed golfer) holds the putter grip in the same way it would hold a pen or pencil.

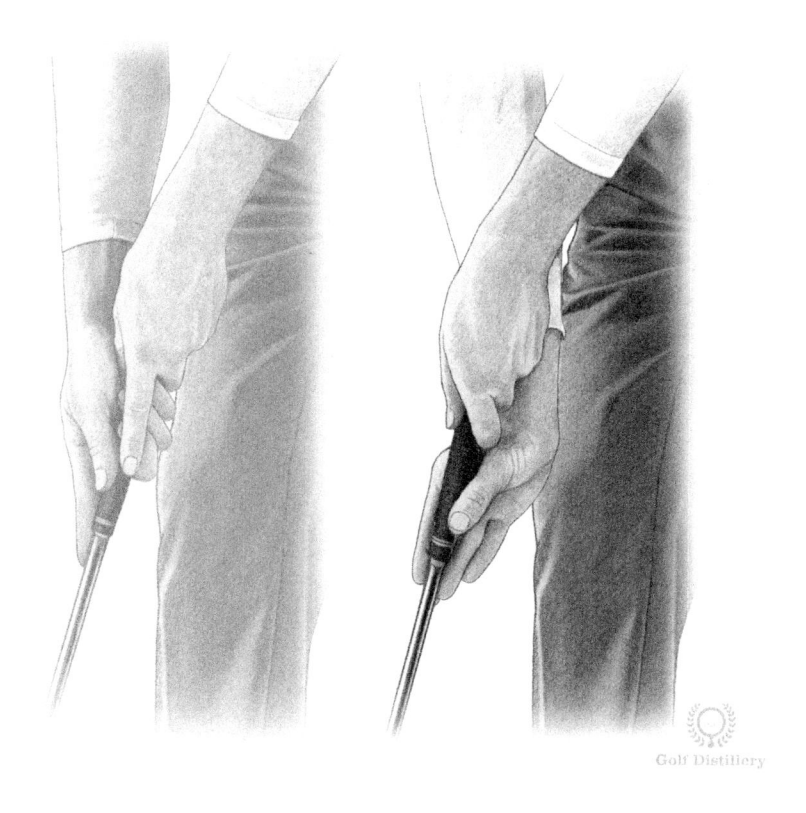

- **Claw Grip**: The right hand makes a claw shape holding the putter grip between the middle fingers.

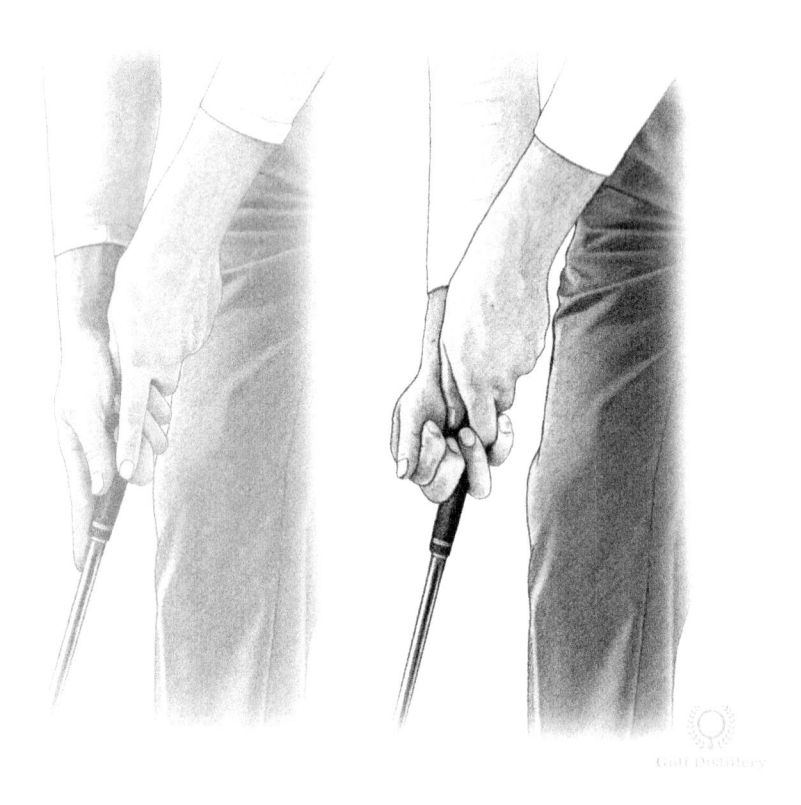

- **Cross-Handed Grip**: This is similar to the traditional overlapping grip, except the hands are switched so that left hand is now lowest on the grip.

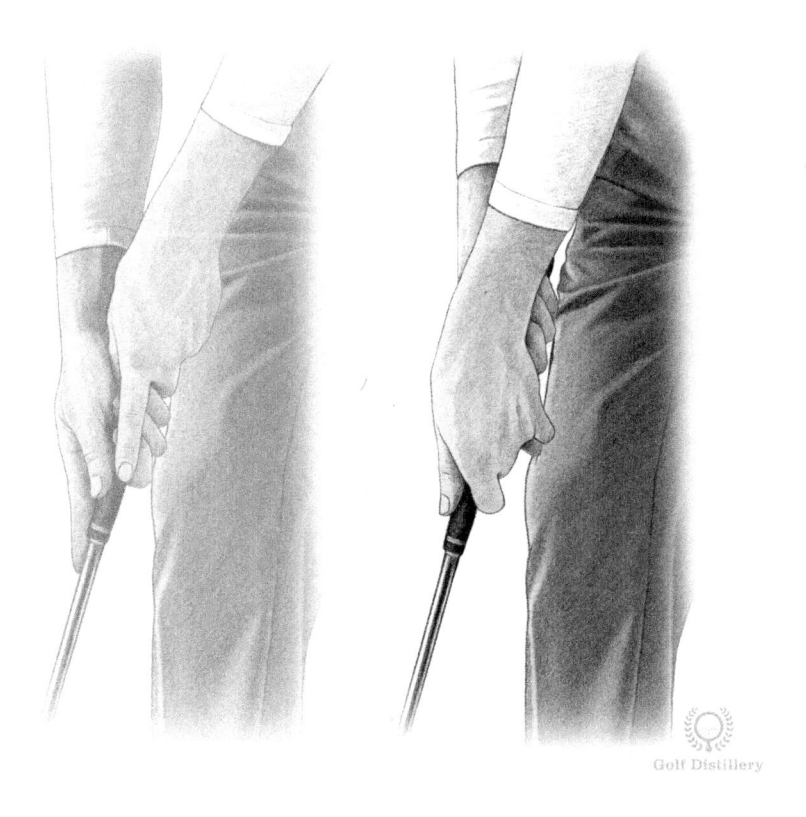

- Although there is no single, best putting grip, all good grips should help to prevent wrist hinge.

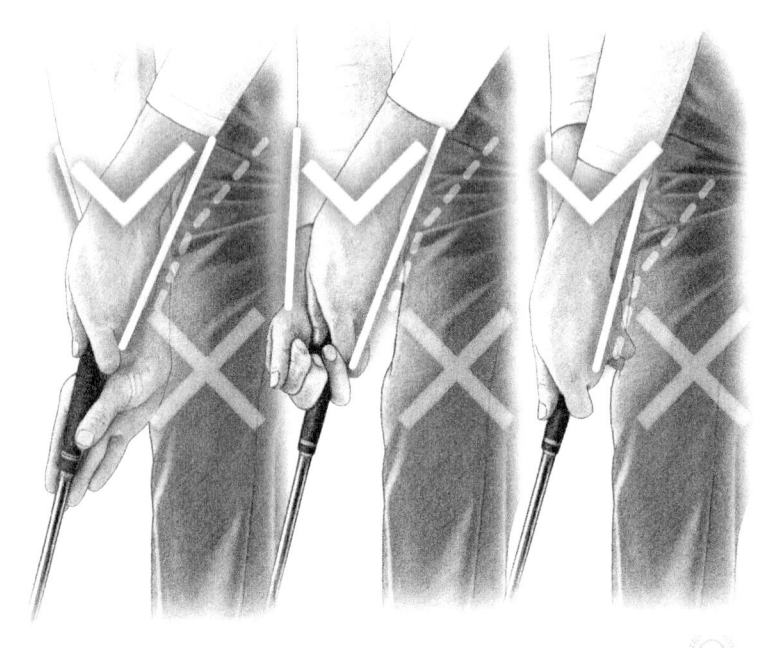

- No matter the grip style you choose the putting stroke is very much a rocking of the shoulders with few other moving parts. Any wrist action will make it difficult for you to consistently control the distances and lines of your putts.

4.8 READING GREENS

This lesson on reading greens should help improve your ability to gauge the break and line of your putts.

It's worth remembering that although reading greens is an important part of good putting, distance control is more important.

A well-paced putt that is roughly on line will never end up more than a few feet away from the hole. A putt that's bang on line but poor for pace usually ends up as a 3-putt, or worse.

With that said, ideally we want the best of both worlds in a great pace and a great line.

• Start assessing a green from a distance as you walk up after hitting your approach shot. Get a feel for the general lie of the land. Notice where the major slopes are, if there are any ponds or drainage run-off areas, etc.

- Getting down low to the ground and behind the golf ball will give you a better perspective to judge the severity and number of breaks facing your putt.

- Try to walk the length of your putt and take a look from behind the hole. Viewing the putt from various angles will give you a much more accurate impression of what's going to happen to the ball.

- Pay particular attention to the second half of the putt. Any slope or break there will have a much greater influence on the ball because it will have slowed down considerably.

- Most handicap golfers under-read big breaking putts by about half. In other words, they'll only hit the ball half as high up the slope as they need to. Therefore, when lining up your putt pick a target that you believe is at the top of the slope or break and focus on hitting your putt to that target.

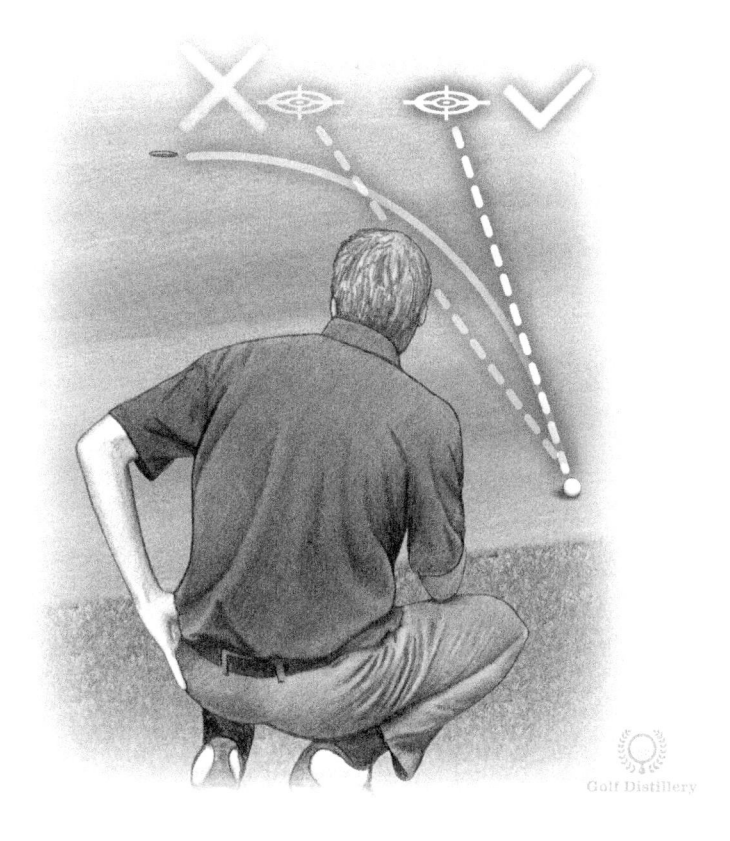

4.9 PUTTING WITH A HYBRID

When the ball is close to the edge of the green — maybe 2-3 feet away — on closely mown grass, many golfers will automatically opt for their putter over a wedge.

And this is something I'd encourage, especially if you're not 100% confident with your chipping game. That's because a poor putt will generally leave you much happier than a poor chip would.

However, if the grass in front of the green is a bit scruffy or if the grass is growing towards the golf ball you might consider using your hybrid or rescue club instead.

- The hybrid is designed so that it doesn't dig into the ground but rather skips nicely through the grass. And it has a bit more loft and weight behind it than a traditional putter. Just enough to get the ball through the first few feet of grass without any trouble.

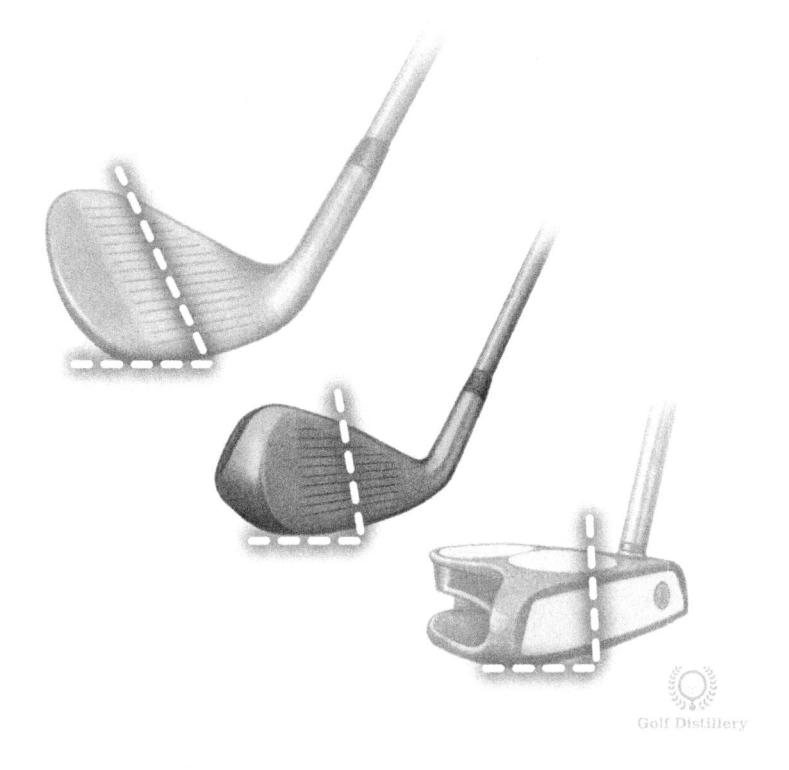

- For this shot we use a combination of a chipping setup — narrow stance, grip right down the club, ball in the middle of the stance, weight forward on to the left side — and a putting stroke.

- So set up like you would for a chip shot and then use a putting stroke — rocking of the shoulders, no wrist hinge, keeping your lower body very still.

4.10 PUTTING DRILL FOR SHORT PUTTS

If you can sink everything from three feet and in you'll really see your scores drop. In conclusion to this putting section (and short game guide) here's a drill to help you do just that.

- Push a tee peg into the back of a practice hole — just above the plastic cup — so that it sticks out about an inch.

- Firstly, this gives you a very specific visual marker to aim for. Even if you miss that very small target chances are the putt will still drop. When playing on the golf course pick a specific mark or spot at the back of the hole and aim for it on your short putts.

- Secondly, imagine that the ball is going to nudge the tee peg back into the earth as if it were a small hammer. This should help you to strike the ball firmly and confidently, taking any break out of the equation in the process.

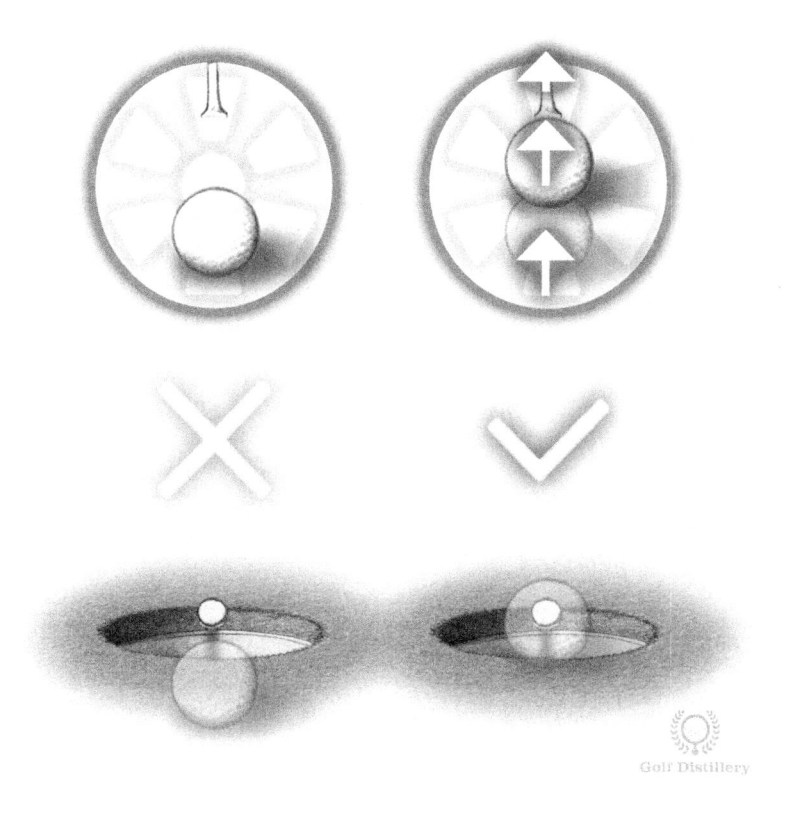

- This is a great little drill to use on the putting green before your competitive rounds. It builds confidence and gets you used to that feeling of being positive over short putts.

YOUTUBE CHANNEL LINK

For more golf tips,
visit our YouTube channel:

Golf Distillery

www.golfdistillery.com

ALSO BY GOLF DISTILLERY

Continue on your quest to better golf with these:

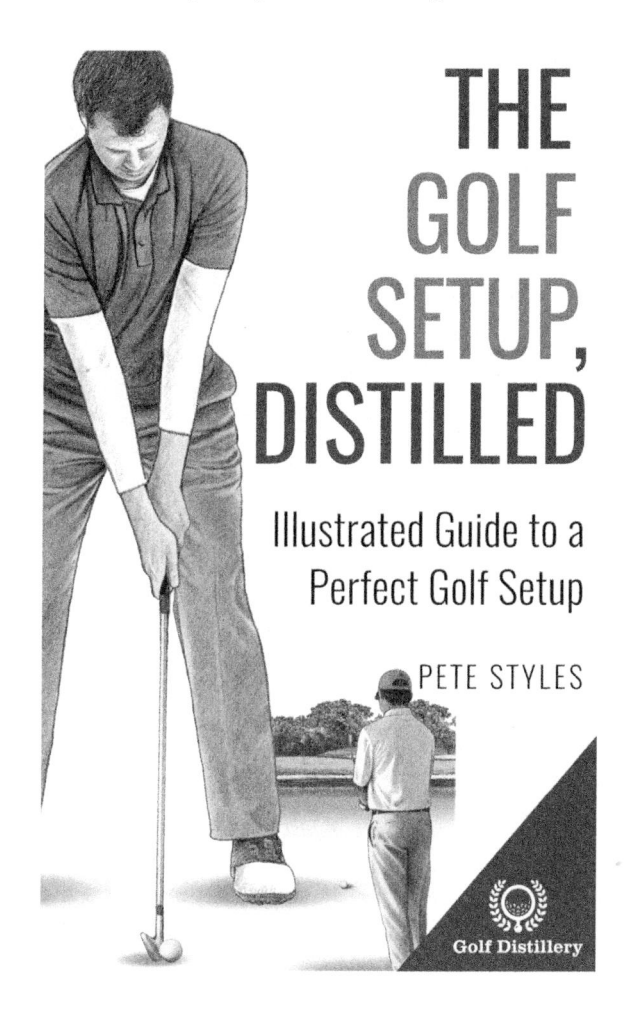

THE GOLF SETUP, DISTILLED

Illustrated Guide to a Perfect Golf Setup

PETE STYLES

Golf Distillery

THE GOLF SWING, DISTILLED

Illustrated Guide to a Proper Golf Swing

PETE STYLES

Golf Distillery

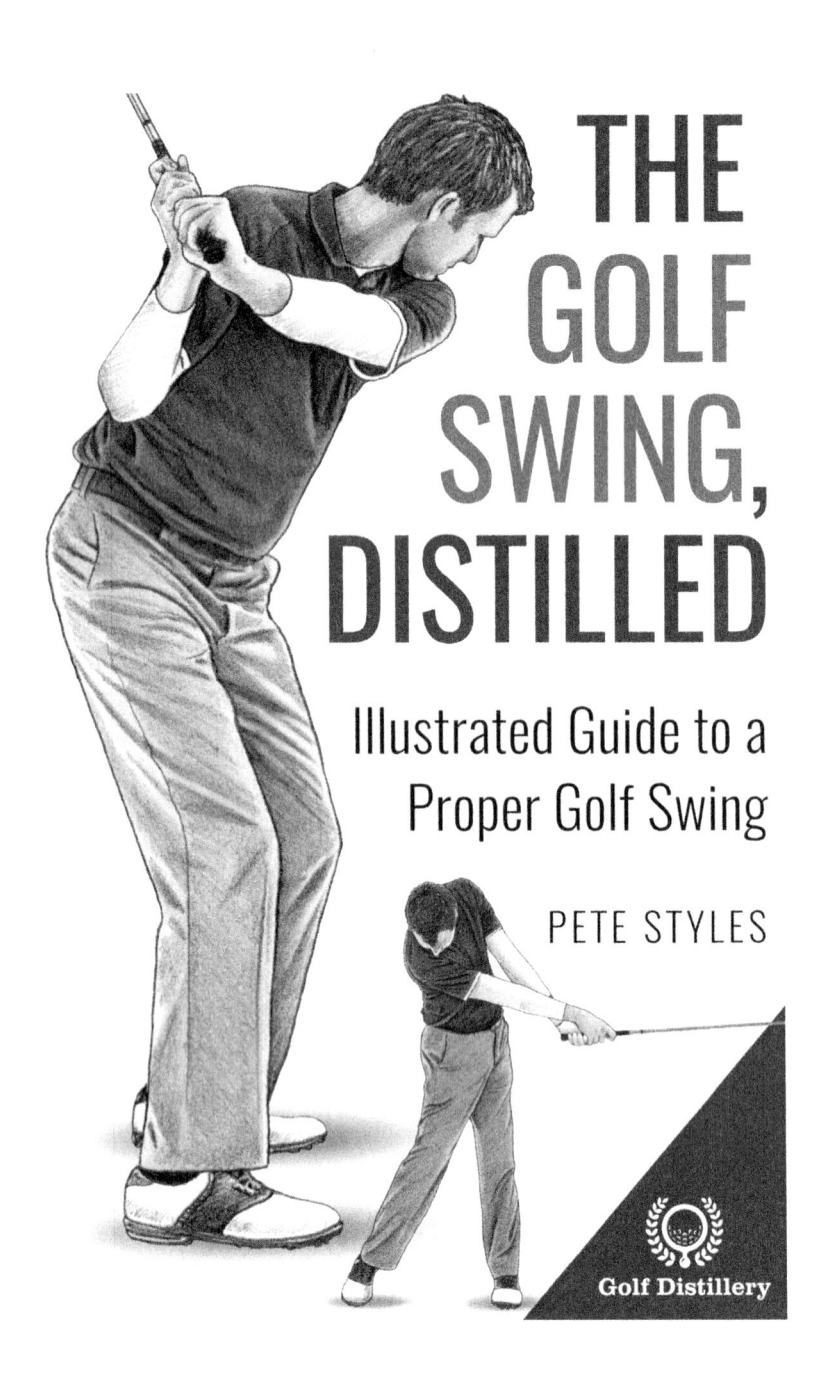

THE GOLF DRILLS, DISTILLED

Illustrated Guide to the Best Golf Drills

PETE STYLES

Golf Distillery

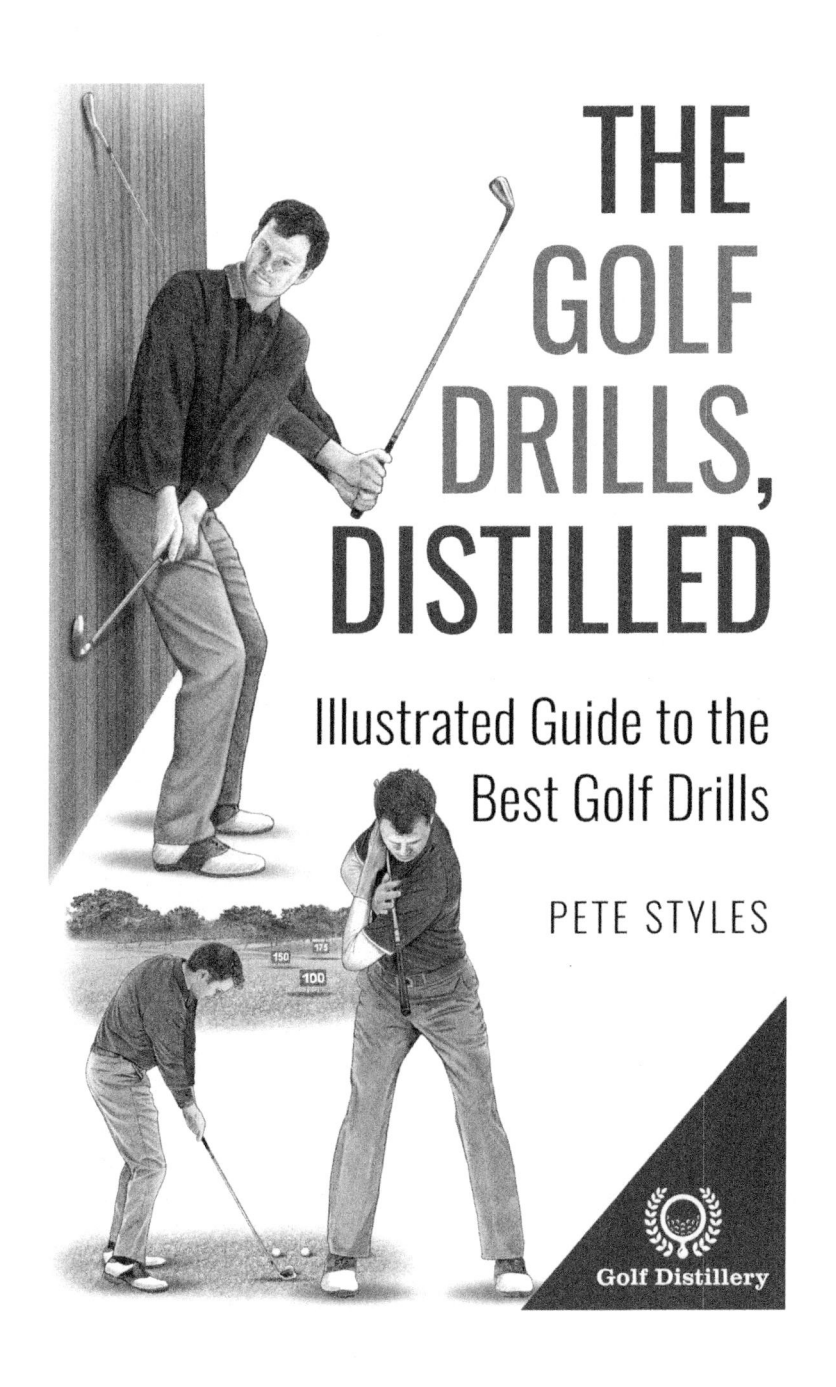

6 WEEKS TO GOLF FITNESS

How to Get Healthy and Fit, and Hit the Ball Further Than Ever

PHIL DAVIES

Golf Distillery

GOLF
THROUGH THE EYES OF A CHILD

Written by
Dominique DeSerres

Illustrated by
Aga Kubish

Golf Distillery

PERSONAL NOTES

PERSONAL NOTES

PERSONAL NOTES

Printed in Dunstable, United Kingdom